The British Aircraft Aerospace Adverts

Compiled By David Robinson
Copyright © David Robinson 2021
All rights reserved
ISBN: 978-1-716-27485-5

Compiler's Notes

The British Aviation Advertisements (1909-1980) series of compilations are designed to provide a handy reference for researchers, enthusiasts and others with an interest in aviation. As such these publications are produced without narrative.

These listings provide an interesting 'linear' method of tracing the evolution of an aviation company, manufacturing process or product line - a product development timeline if you prefer.

All the images featured in this publication are reproduced from original and authentic source material in the Aviation Ancestry collection.

Advertisement sources & credit (Ad Ref:) appear immediately below each item. Ad Ref refers to the record number in the Aviation Ancestry master catalogue & database.

It should be noted that reference sources quoted are not necessarily exclusive. Identical adverts frequently appeared across multiple publications simultaneously, although minor variations in layout might be noted.

Some adverts in a year group may appear at first sight to be identical but closer inspection will normally reveal some subtle change of wording or emphasis.

All items in the catalogue are categorised by year and month. Identical adverts may appear under different year headings but should not be duplicated in any specified year. The absence of adverts in any given month doesn't necessarily mean that none were published as identical adverts may have been published at intervals.

It's worth noting that a surprising number of magazine issues never made it to the newsstand due to industrial disputes of one form or another.

Occasionally some adverts may seem mildly amusing or even offensive to the modern eye but without the inclusion of such material essential historical context would be missing.

Quoted sources represent the best quality original examples or simply the first in the database. Originals may have been printed in full or part colour, unfortunately the cost of publishing these compilations in a richer or full colour format proved to be prohibitive.

It's of interest to note that wartime and immediate post-war publications were subject to government economy restrictions often resulting in poor image quality. Magazines published to a monthly rather than a weekly cycle tended to be of better quality and these are the preferred source for inclusion into these catalogues.

Every effort has been made to produce as complete a reference as possible but inevitably more items will surface from time to time and will be included in future revisions. For latest items the database at aviationancestry.co.uk should be consulted and images requested.

Index

* English Electric aircraft equipment will form part of a dedicated English Electric compilation.

Only the VANGUARD
has this proved flexibility

AIRLINE OPERATORS are invited to look carefully at this diagram and graph, and then compare the Vanguard's flexibility with their own experience of short haul operation on high-density routes.

It is easy to see that this remarkable aircraft can be routed at altitudes of from 5,000 ft to 25,000 ft and above, with practically no penalties in operating costs or speed.

The difference in direct cost between a 500-mile sector flown at 10,000 ft and one flown at an optimum of 20,000 ft is only $44 per trip. A cruising speed of over 400 m.p.h. is available between the height bands of 5,000 ft and 30,000 ft, so that schedules can be maintained irrespective of routeing instructions.

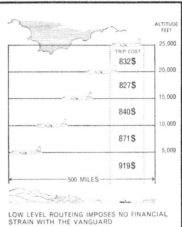

ALTITUDE FEET

TRIP COST
832$ — 25,000
827$ — 20,000
840$ — 15,000
871$ — 10,000
919$ — 5,000

500 MILES

LOW LEVEL ROUTEING IMPOSES NO FINANCIAL STRAIN WITH THE VANGUARD

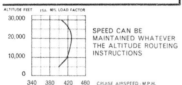

ALTITUDE FEET (ISA. 80% LOAD FACTOR)
30,000
20,000
10,000
0
340 380 420 460 CRUISE AIRSPEED - M.P.H.

SPEED CAN BE MAINTAINED WHATEVER THE ALTITUDE ROUTEING INSTRUCTIONS

Of all the airliners only the Vanguard has all these features

425 m.p.h. cruising • Freight capacity 7/8 tons at normal densities • Full routeing and A.T.C. flexibility • Can use normal existing airfields • Quick turn-round • No airfield noise problems • Ten years' unique Vickers/Rolls-Royce turbo-prop experience . . . *And it is 'Viscount' quiet.*

VICKERS VANGUARD

FOUR ROLLS-ROYCE TYNE TURBO-PROP ENGINES

● *The airliner with the biggest profit potential ever offered to the operator*

VICKERS-ARMSTRONGS (AIRCRAFT) LIMITED   WEYBRIDGE   SURREY

Flight January 1st 1960
Ad Ref 39630

1

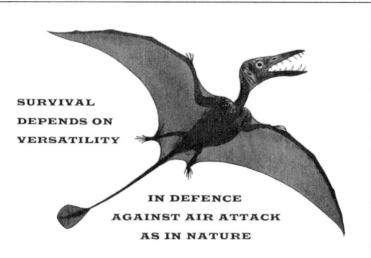

SURVIVAL

DEPENDS ON

VERSATILITY

IN DEFENCE

AGAINST AIR ATTACK

AS IN NATURE

The story of evolution is the story of success, or failure, in versatility. Those animals that could adapt themselves to changing conditions of life multiplied, flourished and survived. Those that were too set in their ways died out.
It is not only in Natural History that versatility – the ability to perform more than one function – is of critical importance. It is equally important in the field of defence against air attack. If we ever again have to defend ourselves against attack from the air, the one certain thing is that the pattern of attack would be chosen so as to make things as difficult as possible for the defence. The less flexible our methods of defence, the more easily they could be baffled.

VERSATILITY IN DEPLOYMENT

A vital weapon for defence against air attack is the guided missile. Missile systems can either be permanently sited on fixed concrete emplacements, or, like the English Electric Thunderbird, be made fully mobile, moved across country in standard military vehicles, and redeployed in a few hours.
The important thing is that the second category – and this means Thunderbird – can also be used in a static role. It can stay put on a chosen site for as long as that site continues to be the most suitable one. It doesn't have to be concreted in: and this saves money and man hours.
But if the unexpected happens – and in war it always does – Thunderbird can be away and in action again to meet a new threat overnight. It is operationally flexible. Now in service with the Army, its inherent mobility allows for quick changes in plan, easy resiting of defence and provides the versatility which is of ever increasing importance to present and future air defence.

EVOLUTION CONTINUES

An even more advanced version has been under development for some time and is well under way. Amongst other improvements, Thunderbird's successor will provide longer range and increased low-level capability whilst still retaining its full mobility and airtransportability. Evolution, in fact, is still going on – an evolution which, as in nature, will still further increase the versatility of the Thunderbird Weapon system, upon which our survival may depend.

'ENGLISH ELECTRIC' THUNDERBIRD

ENGLISH ELECTRIC AVIATION LIMITED · GUIDED WEAPONS DIVISION · LUTON · STEVENAGE · WOOMERA

A MEMBER OF THE ENGLISH ELECTRIC AVIATION GROUP

GW 53

Flight January 8th 1960
Ad Ref 39506

V810 AIRCRAFT-MILE COSTS
II cents below forecast!
−That's proof of
𝕍𝕀𝕊ℂ𝕆𝕌ℕ𝕋
Economy for you!

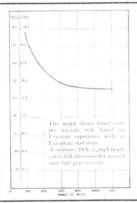

After 6 months' V810 operation
CONTINENTAL AIRLINES REPORT

• *Aircraft mile cost 71.33 cents for an average sector of 500 miles*
 — 11 CENTS BELOW FORECAST !

• *Outstanding V810 economy and passenger appeal brought the airline $1.3 MILLIONS in Viscount profit between May and December 1958. Average fleet of nine aircraft for the period.*

The Viscount V810 is still without a challenger in its class as a modern, medium-sized short/medium haul airliner. Its economy, flexibility, 365 m.p.h. cruise speed, and background of Vickers engineering and Rolls-Royce turbo-prop experience in over 370 Viscounts in service all over the world, make it unique as a profit-earner in this field.

Low fare/High profit note

The V810 in a 70-seat layout has a seat-mile cost of only 1.34 cents at 300 miles, and a proved 1.01 cents at 500 miles. *With only 49 passengers, this aircraft would clear 10% profit at fares 15% down on current U.S.A. coach fares!*

**Promised V810 economy
more than proved in practice!**
The economical performance promised by this graph has been more than fulfilled in the first six months' operation of Continental Airlines' V810 fleet.

VICKERS 𝕍𝕀𝕊ℂ𝕆𝕌ℕ𝕋 𝟠𝟙𝟘
FOUR ROLLS-ROYCE DART TURBO-PROP ENGINES

• *Fastest and most economical medium-sized airliner in the world*

VICKERS-ARMSTRONGS (AIRCRAFT) LIMITED WEYBRIDGE SURREY

Flight January 15th 1960
Ad Ref 39641

3

Interavia February 1960
Ad Ref 82094

4

ADAPTABILITY IS ESSENTIAL TO SURVIVAL

AGAINST AIR ATTACK AS IN NATURE

Only animals versatile enough to withstand Nature's ever-changing threats have survived and flourish today. Those like the pareiasaurus which could not adapt themselves to varying conditions have gradually become extinct.

So, too, when it comes to defence against air attack, a system that is not flexible is a hostage to fortune – for to believe that the attack will conform to an expected pattern would be foolhardy in the extreme.

DEFENCE MUST BE FLEXIBLE

Our defence, in which guided weapons will play a highly important part, must be flexible – must be prepared for danger at any point and from any direction. So when English Electric designed and constructed the Thunderbird ground-to-air guided missile, they built flexibility into it from the start. It was made capable of operating permanently from one site like any other fixed installation for as long as it was needed there. But, should the need arise, it could quickly be moved to meet whatever threat might develop.

The operating system was developed, using standard military vehicles, in such a way that overnight – in a few hours – it could be redeployed and in action again where most needed to meet a new threat.

PRODUCTION AND DEVELOPMENT

Thunderbird is unique. It can be used in both a static and a mobile role. It has passed its service trials and is in production. Now in service with the Army, its inherent mobility allows easy resiting of defence and provides the flexibility which is of ever increasing importance to present and future air defence.

And evolution is still going on. An even more advanced Thunderbird is well under way. Employing advanced techniques and retaining its full mobility, the new version will, among other things, provide increased low-level capability and increased range.

'ENGLISH ELECTRIC' THUNDERBIRD

ENGLISH ELECTRIC AVIATION LIMITED · GUIDED WEAPONS DIVISION · LUTON · STEVENAGE · WOOMERA

A MEMBER OF THE ENGLISH ELECTRIC AVIATION GROUP

GW. 25

Flight February 5th 1960
Ad Ref 39505

5

Flight February 12th 1960
Ad Ref 39628

The British Aircraft Corporation Aerospace Adverts 1960-1977

Flight February 26th 1960
Ad Ref 39489

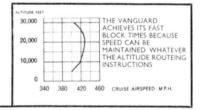
Flight February 26th 1960
Ad Ref 39629

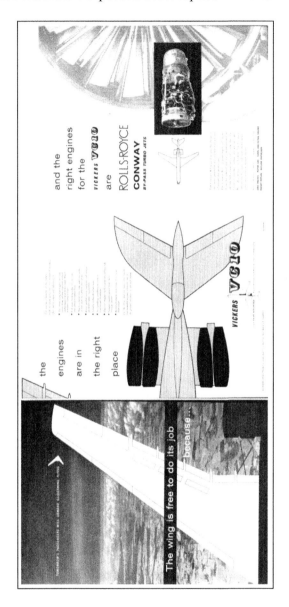

Flight March 11th 1960
Ad Ref 39635

BY DAY OR NIGHT, IN ANY WEATHER...

The ENGLISH ELECTRIC Lightning provides front-line defence at all times. It is completely equipped with navigational, radar and automatic aids. Whatever the weather, in daylight or darkness, the pilot can make full and effective use of the Lightning's stupendous performance.

...THE *LIGHTNING*

IS INCOMPARABLE

'ENGLISH ELECTRIC'
aircraft

ENGLISH ELECTRIC AVIATION LIMITED · MARCONI HOUSE · STRAND · WC2

A MEMBER OF THE **ENGLISH ELECTRIC** AVIATION GROUP

Flight March 18th 1960
Ad Ref 39491

SURVIVAL, FOR US AS FOR THE CHAMELEON, DEMANDS VERSATILITY

You cannot take a chameleon by surprise. It can always adapt itself to the prevailing conditions. It owes its survival to this adaptability. The same principle applies in modern warfare. A defence system which is flexible in application is less likely to be defeated than one which is not.

A MISSILE THAT DOES TWO JOBS

Thunderbird can be used in two ways. It can be used efficiently in a static role operating from a preselected site for as long as it is tactically required there, and it needs no concreting-in. It can also be rapidly redeployed to meet some new threat should the need arise – and attack seldom hits us where we are expecting it.

Thunderbird can be moved easily and quickly – on wheels or by air. Now in service with the Army and designed round standard service vehicles it can be redeployed and in action where most needed within hours. Its inherent mobility and air transportability provides that flexibility which is of ever increasing importance in present and future air defence.

NEW DEVELOPMENTS

And evolution still goes on. Already the successor to Thunderbird has been under development for some considerable time. Using the latest techniques and retaining its full mobility, the new version will provide, among other things, increased low-level capability and longer range.

The Chameleon has survived because its versatile defence gives protection anywhere. Our own survival may equally depend on similar versatility.

'ENGLISH ELECTRIC' THUNDERBIRD

ENGLISH ELECTRIC AVIATION LIMITED · GUIDED WEAPONS DIVISION · LUTON · STEVENAGE · WOOMERA

A MEMBER OF THE ENGLISH ELECTRIC AVIATION GROUP

Aeroplane March 25th 1960
Ad Ref 3617

11

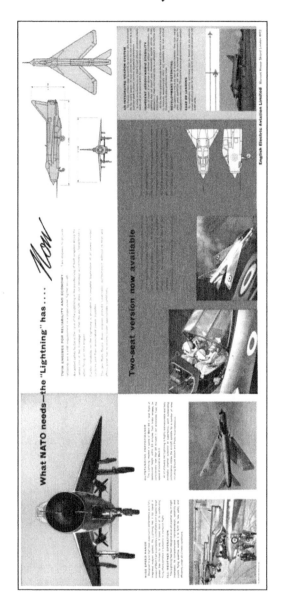

Aeroplane March 25th 1960
Ad Ref 3645

AS A FULLY-INTEGRATED WEAPON...

Everything connected with the flying and the operating
of the ENGLISH ELECTRIC Lightning was designed and developed
as a co-ordinated system. The airframe, the engines, the
radar equipment, the electronic aids, the armament, the fire
control devices—all were planned from the start to make
the Lightning safe for its pilot, and deadly for its target.

...THE *LIGHTNING*

IS INCOMPARABLE

'ENGLISH ELECTRIC' aircraft

ENGLISH ELECTRIC AVIATION LIMITED
MARCONI HOUSE · STRAND · WC2

Flight April 22nd 1960
Ad Ref 39488

13

British Aviation Industry Advertisements

Flight May 20th 1960
Ad Ref 39643

14

Flight June 3rd 1960
Ad Ref 39397

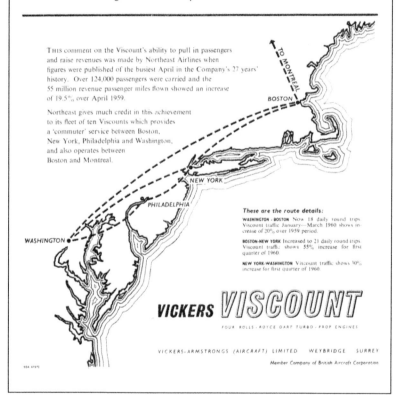

Northeast Airlines praise Viscount contribution to record April figures

'Strong Public Acceptance of the Viscount'

THIS comment on the Viscount's ability to pull in passengers and raise revenues was made by Northeast Airlines when figures were published of the busiest April in the Company's 27 years' history. Over 124,000 passengers were carried and the 55 million revenue passenger miles flown showed an increase of 19.5% over April 1959.

Northeast gives much credit in this achievement to its fleet of ten Viscounts which provides a 'commuter' service between Boston, New York, Philadelphia and Washington, and also operates between Boston and Montreal.

These are the route details:

WASHINGTON - BOSTON Now 18 daily round trips. Viscount traffic January—March 1960 shows increase of 20% over 1959 period.

BOSTON-NEW YORK Increased to 21 daily round trips. Viscount traffic shows 55% increase for first quarter of 1960.

NEW YORK-WASHINGTON Viscount traffic shows 30% increase for first quarter of 1960.

VICKERS VISCOUNT

FOUR ROLLS-ROYCE DART TURBO-PROP ENGINES

VICKERS-ARMSTRONGS (AIRCRAFT) LIMITED   WEYBRIDGE   SURREY

Member Company of British Aircraft Corporation

Flight June 24th 1960
Ad Ref 39642

16

Flight June 24th 1960
Ad Ref 39490

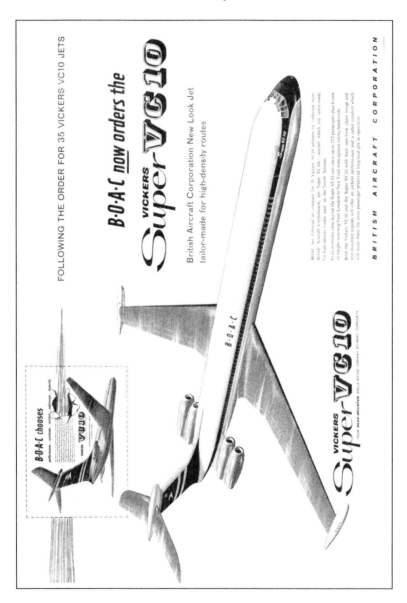

Flight July 8th 1960
Ad Ref 39634

44

AIRLINES HAVE CHOSEN . . . VISCOUNT

All-Nippon Airways of Tokyo — three Viscount 810's ordered! Ghana Airways — three also! This now makes forty-four airlines with Viscounts in service or on order, as listed opposite. Five Governments and seven private companies or individuals also operate Viscounts.

22

HAVE RE-ORDERED . . . VISCOUNT

Of these forty-four airlines, twenty-two have now placed repeat orders for Viscounts.

2,500,000

HOURS HAVE BEEN FLOWN BY . . . VISCOUNT

This impressive total includes half a million revenue hours flown by BEA up to April 1960.

EUROPE
British European Airways
Air France
Aer Lingus
K.L.M.
Lufthansa
Alitalia
Austrian Airlines
Turkish Airlines
Airwork
Hunting Clan Air Transport
Tradair
Transair
Eagle Aviation
Icelandair

NORTH AMERICA
Capital Airlines
Continental Airlines
Northeast Airlines
Trans-Canada Air Lines
Maritime Central Airways

CENTRAL AND SOUTH AMERICA AND CARIBBEAN
Vasp (Brazil)
Pluna (Uruguay)
L.A.V. (Venezuela)

VISCOUNT
FOUR ROLLS-ROYCE DART TURBO-PROP ENGINES

Lloyd Aereo Colombiano
TACA (El Salvador)
British West Indian Airways
Cubana

MIDDLE EAST
Middle East Airlines
Misrair (Egypt)
Iraqi Airways
Iranian Airways
Kuwait Airways

AFRICA
Central African Airways
Sudan Airways
South African Airways
Ghana Airways

SOUTH EAST ASIA
Indian Airlines Corporation
Pakistan International Air Lines
Union of Burma Airways
Malayan Airways

AUSTRALASIA
Trans-Australia Airlines
Ansett-A.N.A.
New Zealand National Airlines Corporation

PACIFIC
Philippine Air Lines
All Nippon Airways

VICKERS-ARMSTRONGS (AIRCRAFT) LIMITED WEYBRIDGE SURREY
MEMBER COMPANY OF BRITISH AIRCRAFT CORPORATION

Flight August 5th 1960
Ad Ref 39639

19

British Aviation Industry Advertisements

Flight August 12th 1960
Ad Ref 39640

20

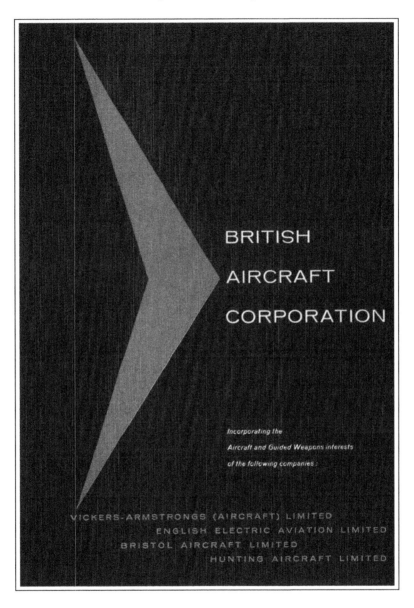

Flight September 2nd 1960
Ad Ref 39398

British Aviation Industry Advertisements

The English Electric all-weather day and night interceptor, one of the most advanced aircraft in the world, is the fastest British aircraft in production, capable of flying at more than twice the speed of sound. The Lightning has been ordered for the Royal Air Force in substantial quantities and is now in service.

ENGLISH ELECTRIC AVIATION LIMITED · MARCONI HOUSE · STRAND · LONDON WC2

MEMBER COMPANY OF BRITISH AIRCRAFT CORPORATION

Flight September 2nd 1960
Ad Ref 39494

Flight September 2nd 1960
Ad Ref 39508

Flight September 2nd 1960
Ad Ref 39637

Flight September 9th 1960
Ad Ref 39399

EVEN BETTER THAN PROMISED

Before the first Vanguard goes into scheduled service, and little more than a year after the first flight tests, development has made possible dramatic increases in maximum operating weights. Details are given in the table below. These improvements have been achieved for an empty weight increase of only 600 lb, and allow a margin of 1,600 lb for future development, equipment changes or customers' special requirements.

VANGUARD PAYLOAD UP BY 8,000 lb

	Original specification	New specification	Increase
GROSS TAKE-OFF WEIGHT	141,000 lb	146,500 lb	5,500 lb
MAX. LANDING WEIGHT	121,000 lb	130,500 lb	9,500 lb
MAX. 'ZERO FUEL' WEIGHT	112,500 lb	122,500 lb	10,000 lb
MAX. PAYLOAD	29,000 lb	37,000 lb	8,000 lb

The Vanguard can now carry 139 economy-class passengers plus over 8,000 lb freight. Without intermediate refuelling, 100-passenger payloads can be carried over such important consecutive sectors as London–Frankfurt–Vienna–Prague. Operators with profit in mind and air travel for all in view, will find the Vanguard is more attractive than ever.

VICKERS VANGUARD

FOUR ROLLS-ROYCE TYNE PROPELLER-TURBINE ENGINES

The airliner with the biggest profit potential ever offered to the operator

VICKERS-ARMSTRONGS (AIRCRAFT) LIMITED WEYBRIDGE SURREY
Member Company of BRITISH AIRCRAFT CORPORATION

Flight September 16th 1960
Ad Ref 39632

Flight September 23rd 1960
Ad Ref 39638

AS A PIECE OF APPLIED AERODYNAMICS...

Over the whole of its phenomenal speed range—far more than 10 to 1—from its moderate landing speed, through subsonic and transonic speeds, up to its very considerably supersonic maximum, the ENGLISH ELECTRIC Lightning is inherently aerodynamically stable. Without any assistance from electronics it is at all speeds free from pitch-up.

...THE *LIGHTNING*

IS INCOMPARABLE

ENGLISH ELECTRIC AVIATION LTD
ENGLISH ELECTRIC HOUSE · STRAND · WC2

MEMBER COMPANY OF BRITISH AIRCRAFT CORPORATION

Flight September 30th 1960
Ad Ref 39493

*Profit from
cheaper fares
with the...*

...*VICKERS*

VANGUARD

FOUR ROLLS-ROYCE TYNE TURBO-PROP ENGINES

VICKERS-ARMSTRONGS (AIRCRAFT) LIMITED WEYBRIDGE SURREY

Aeroplane Directory 1960 Edition
Ad Ref 87336

HAY...

A meadow –
of no military significance.
Not far away a vital military area.

...PRESTO!

A convoy arrived
Thunderbird deployed in less than an hour.
The defence requirement changed
Thunderbird moves rapidly to where next needed
A meadow remains

The English Electric THUNDERBIRD is:
The standard Army A.A. guided weapon
Completely mobile
Easily assembled and serviced
Being developed with C.W. techniques
giving improved range and more effective
low level cover and now in final proving stage.

'ENGLISH ELECTRIC'
THUNDERBIRD

English Electric Aviation Ltd
Guided Weapons Division   Luton · Stevenage · Woomera

MEMBER COMPANY OF BRITISH AIRCRAFT CORPORATION

Flight October 7th 1960
Ad Ref 39507

30

Flight October 7th 1960
Ad Ref 39636

31

By our standards, a thousandth of an inch is an agricultural idea

You know about the man who was asked how big a 'thou' was? 'Very, very small' he said. He was asked how many there were in an inch. 'Millions of them' he said.

In this unusual factory of ours—unique in Europe, we suppose—we don't think of a 'thou' as at all small. We have had to train ourselves to take a tolerance of half a tenth in our stride, and to use on our production inspection-line a machine that will measure out-of-roundness of the order of one millionth of an inch.

But then we are in production with instruments the like of which the world has never seen before. We produce (in partnership with Minneapolis Honeywell) Inertial Quality Gyroscopes so accurate that they precess less than half a degree *per day*, so sensitive that you can use them for finding true North to within a few minutes of arc. Small wonder that we do 'sand'-blasting with bicarbonate of soda, and that a speck of dust is a calamity.

'ENGLISH ELECTRIC'
INERTIAL GUIDANCE

INSTRUMENT WING · GUIDED WEAPONS DIVISION · ENGLISH ELECTRIC AVIATION LIMITED · STEVENAGE
Member Company of British Aircraft Corporation

Flight October 14th 1960
Ad Ref 39500

Flight October 21st 1960
Ad Ref 39631

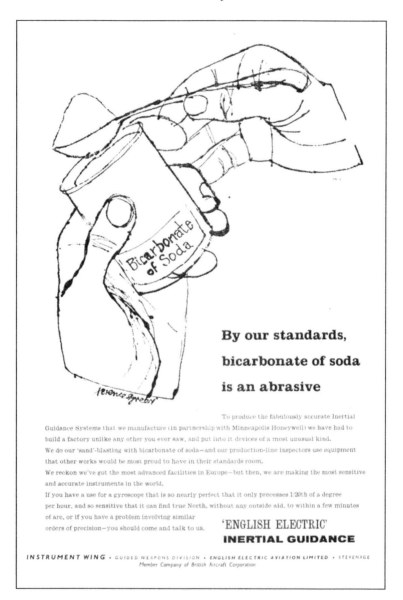

By our standards,

bicarbonate of soda

is an abrasive

To produce the fabulously accurate Inertial Guidance Systems that we manufacture (in partnership with Minneapolis Honeywell) we have had to build a factory unlike any other you ever saw, and put into it devices of a most unusual kind.

We do our 'sand'-blasting with bicarbonate of soda—and our production-line inspectors use equipment that other works would be most proud to have in their standards room.

We reckon we've got the most advanced facilities in Europe—but then, we are making the most sensitive and accurate instruments in the world.

If you have a use for a gyroscope that is so nearly perfect that it only precesses 1/20th of a degree per hour, and so sensitive that it can find true North, without any outside aid, to within a few minutes of arc, or if you have a problem involving similar orders of precision—you should come and talk to us.

'ENGLISH ELECTRIC'

INERTIAL GUIDANCE

INSTRUMENT WING · GUIDED WEAPONS DIVISION · **ENGLISH ELECTRIC AVIATION LIMITED** · STEVENAGE
Member Company of British Aircraft Corporation

Flight October 28th 1960
Ad Ref 39501

34

WHY THE *LIGHTNING* IS INCOMPARABLE

All-weather operation. The aircraft can operate by day or night in all weathers. It has full navigational, flying and landing aids, airborne search and track radar.

An integrated weapon system. The airframe, its components, engines, armament, fire control system and other equipment have been developed to work together as a co-ordinated whole.

Flexibility. The aircraft has a wide speed and performance range. Alternative armament and other auxiliaries give it great versatility.

Inherent aerodynamic stability. The aircraft is fully supersonic yet inherently aerodynamically stable.

Twin engines for safety and economy. The installation of twin engines enables complete duplication of all power control systems and the power supply for them. At the same time it gives supersonic performance without re-heat and affords considerable fuel economy under appropriate conditions.

Development potential. The basic design has great potential for development, not only in performance, but also in adaptation to other roles.

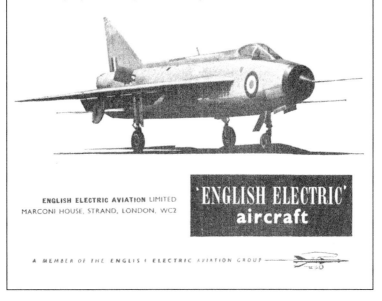

ENGLISH ELECTRIC AVIATION LIMITED
MARCONI HOUSE, STRAND, LONDON, WC2

'ENGLISH ELECTRIC'
aircraft

A MEMBER OF THE ENGLISH ELECTRIC AVIATION GROUP

Aeroplane Directory 1960
Edition Ad Ref 87331

FOR ITS FUTURE DEVELOPMENT POSSIBILITIES...

The ENGLISH ELECTRIC Lightning is one of the most advanced fighters in the world. Even so the basic design has further great potential development—not only in performance, but also in adaptation to other operational roles. This built-in stretch offers economies of production and operation as well as ensuring that, tactically speaking, it can be adapted to meet any situation which may arise.

...THE LIGHTNING

IS INCOMPARABLE

ENGLISH ELECTRIC AVIATION LTD
ENGLISH ELECTRIC HOUSE · STRAND · WC2

MEMBER COMPANY OF BRITISH AIRCRAFT CORPORATION

Flight November 11th 1960
Ad Ref 39492

A FIELD IS A FIELD IS A...

A field down some country lane of no military significance—until a military formation asks for air defence

...GUIDED WEAPON SITE

A battery equipped with the Thunderbird A.A. Guided Weapon arrives—it came in standard service vehicles across country—it deployed in less than an hour—the air defence has been provided • The nearby military formation moves on; so does the Thunderbird battery.

The English Electric THUNDERBIRD is:

• The standard Army A.A. guided weapon   • Completely mobile by land and air   • Rugged and of proven reliability   • Easily assembled and serviced in the field   • Being developed with C.W. techniques giving improved range and more effective low-level cover and now in final proving stage.

ENGLISH ELECTRIC THUNDERBIRD

English Electric Aviation Ltd · Guided Weapons Division Luton · Stevenage · Woomera

A COMPANY OF **BRITISH AIRCRAFT CORPORATION**

Aeroplane November 18th 1960
Ad Ref 39504

37

Flight December 2nd 1960
Ad Ref 39633

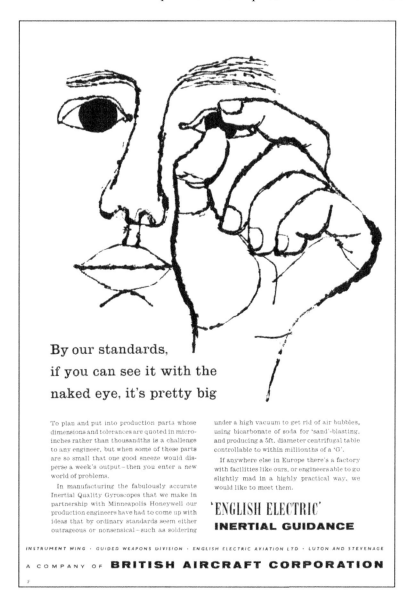

By our standards,
if you can see it with the
naked eye, it's pretty big

To plan and put into production parts whose dimensions and tolerances are quoted in micro-inches rather than thousandths is a challenge to any engineer, but when some of these parts are so small that one good sneeze would disperse a week's output – then you enter a new world of problems.

In manufacturing the fabulously accurate Inertial Quality Gyroscopes that we make in partnership with Minneapolis Honeywell our production engineers have had to come up with ideas that by ordinary standards seem either outrageous or nonsensical – such as soldering under a high vacuum to get rid of air bubbles, using bicarbonate of soda for 'sand'-blasting, and producing a 5ft. diameter centrifugal table controllable to within millionths of a 'G'.

If anywhere else in Europe there's a factory with facilities like ours, or engineers able to go slightly mad in a highly practical way, we would like to meet them.

'ENGLISH ELECTRIC'
INERTIAL GUIDANCE

INSTRUMENT WING · GUIDED WEAPONS DIVISION · ENGLISH ELECTRIC AVIATION LTD · LUTON AND STEVENAGE

A COMPANY OF **BRITISH AIRCRAFT CORPORATION**

F

Flight December 9th 1960
Ad Ref 39497

39

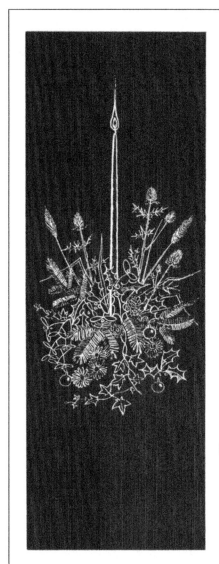

With warmest
good wishes
for Christmas
and the New Year
from
**BRITISH
AIRCRAFT
CORPORATION**

Flight December 16th 1960
Ad Ref 39400

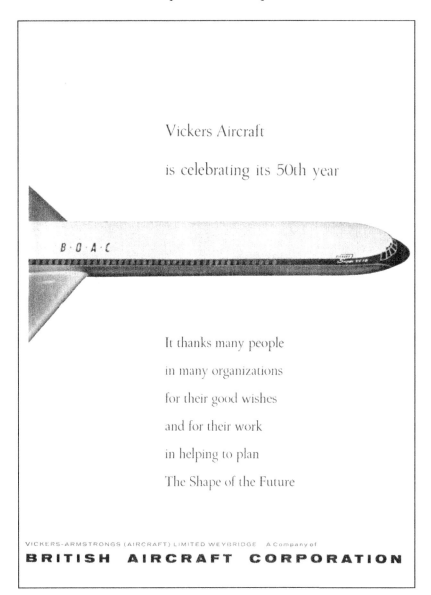

Vickers Aircraft

is celebrating its 50th year

B·O·A·C

It thanks many people

in many organizations

for their good wishes

and for their work

in helping to plan

The Shape of the Future

VICKERS-ARMSTRONGS (AIRCRAFT) LIMITED WEYBRIDGE   A Company of

BRITISH AIRCRAFT CORPORATION

Flight January 6th 1961
Ad Ref 15220

Aeroplane January 27th 1961
Ad Ref 15213

42

Aeroplane January 27th 1961
Ad Ref 15219

BRITISH
AIRCRAFT
CORPORATION

The new force in world aviation

The four member companies of British Aircraft Corporation have, since the war, constructed over 5,000 aircraft of all types. This number includes: **500 Four-Engined Turbine Airliners 900 Twin and Four Jet Bombers 1,700 Jet Fighters 1,100 Trainers** The aircraft now being built or developed within British Aircraft Corporation include VC10 and BAC-107 rear-engined jetliners, Vanguard and Viscount turbo-prop airliners, Canberra jet bombers, Lightning and TSR-2 supersonic military aircraft, the Jet Provost trainer, the T-188 all-steel supersonic research aircraft and a project study for a supersonic airliner * Guided weapons produced by British Aircraft Corporation include Bloodhound, Thunderbird, Blue Water and Vigilant * British Aircraft Corporation combines the aircraft and guided weapons interests of :

Bristol Aircraft Limited   English Electric Aviation Limited
Vickers-Armstrongs (Aircraft) Limited   Hunting Aircraft Limited

Together these famous companies have fashioned a powerful new force in world aviation. It is backed by great resources and by a confidence, an experience, and a knowledge unique to an organisation whose aircraft are today in service with 50 airlines and with the armed services of 28 nations.

Aeroplane January 27th 1961
Ad Ref 15226

44

BRITISH AIRCRAFT CORPORATION

ONE HUNDRED PALL MALL LONDON SW1 ENGLAND

The four member companies of British Aircraft Corporation have, since the war, constructed over 5,000 aircraft of all types * This number includes:

500 Four-Engined Turbine Airliners
900 Twin and Four Jet Bombers
1,700 Jet Fighters 1,100 Trainers

The aircraft now being built or developed within British Aircraft Corporation include VC10, Super VC10 and BAC-107 rear engined jetliners, Vanguard and Viscount turbo-prop airliners, Canberra jet bombers, Lightning and TSR-2 supersonic military aircraft, the Jet Provost trainer, the T-188 all-steel supersonic research aircraft and a project study for a supersonic airliner * Guided weapons produced by British Aircraft Corporation include Bloodhound, Thunderbird, Blue Water and Vigilant.

British Aircraft Corporation combines the aircraft and guided weapons interests of:

Vickers-Armstrongs (Aircraft) Limited
English Electric Aviation Limited
Bristol Aircraft Limited
Hunting Aircraft Limited

Together these famous companies have fashioned a powerful new force in world aviation. It is backed by great resources and by a confidence, an experience, and a knowledge unique to an organisation whose aircraft are today in service with 50 airlines and with the armed services of 28 nations.

BRITISH
AIRCRAFT
CORPORATION

The new force
in world aviation

Aeronautics February 1961
Ad Ref 61588

45

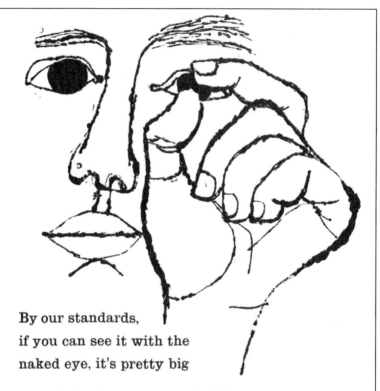

By our standards,
if you can see it with the
naked eye, it's pretty big

To plan and put into production parts whose dimensions and tolerances are quoted in micro-inches rather than thousandths is a challenge to any engineer, but when some of these parts are so small that one good sneeze would disperse a week's output – then you enter a new world of problems.

In manufacturing the fabulously accurate Inertial Quality Gyroscopes that we make in partnership with Minneapolis Honeywell our production engineers have had to come up with ideas that by ordinary standards seem either outrageous or nonsensical – such as soldering under a high vacuum to get rid of air bubbles, using bicarbonate of soda for 'sand'-blasting, and producing a 5ft. diameter centrifugal table controllable to within millionths of a 'G'.

If anywhere else in Europe there's a factory with facilities like ours, or engineers able to go slightly mad in a highly practical way, we would like to meet them.

'ENGLISH ELECTRIC'
INERTIAL GUIDANCE

INSTRUMENT WING · GUIDED WEAPONS DIVISION · ENGLISH ELECTRIC AVIATION LTD · LUTON AND STEVENAGE

A COMPANY OF

BRITISH AIRCRAFT CORPORATION
ONE HUNDRED PALL MALL LONDON SW1

Flight February 3rd 1961
Ad Ref 15231

46

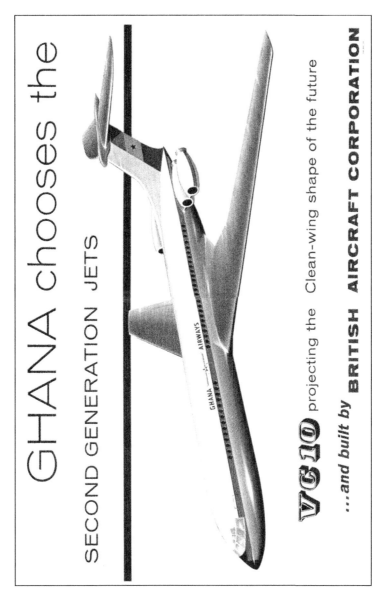

Flight February 17th 1961
Ad Ref 15221

47

...ordered for The Royal Air Force

During a recent speech, Britain's Minister of Defence, Mr. Harold Watkinson, said of TSR-2...

■ STOL
■ Long range at Mach 2 or better
■ Wide range of weapons
■ Great flexibility of roles
■ High accuracy navigation/attack system

'One of the principal features of TSR-2 will be its ability to operate at high speeds and at extremely low altitudes .... an automatic terrain following device will enable the aircraft to approach its target beneath enemy radar cover. It should be practically invuiner-able to all known forms of counter-attack .... As far as is known, this low altitude performance is not matched by any other aircraft in the world at the present time.'

Powered by Bristol Siddeley Olympus Turbo-jets

BRITISH AIRCRAFT CORPORATION
ONE HUNDRED PALL MALL LONDON SW1

Flight February 17th 1961
Ad Ref 15224

48

Flight March 10th 1961
Ad Ref 15218

The most advanced tactical strike reconnaissance aircraft in the world. Ordered for The Royal Air Force

...and built by

BRITISH AIRCRAFT CORPORATION

Flight March 10th 1961
Ad Ref 15225

VICKERS **VIGILANT** One-man anti-tank missile easily carried into action by infantryman or paratrooper. The Vigilant's gyro-stabilised velocity guidance system gives greatest accuracy, widest range band, lowest training costs and easiest control.

ENGLISH ELECTRIC **THUNDERBIRD** A fully mobile, solid-fuel, air-transportable ground-to-air missile in service with the British Army. A development contract has been placed for Thunderbird Mark II.

4 GUIDED MISSILES FOR WESTERN DEFENCE

BRISTOL/FERRANTI **BLOODHOUND** A long-range, high-altitude, ram-jet powered, ground-to-air missile adopted by the Royal Air Force, Sweden & Australia. Bloodhound Mark II is now under full development.

ENGLISH ELECTRIC **BLUE WATER** This tactical surface-to-surface weapon is Britain's second-generation army missile. It has a solid-fuel motor, inertial guidance, high accuracy, rapid fire power and great mobility.

AND BUILT BY
BRITISH AIRCRAFT CORPORATION
ONE HUNDRED PALL MALL LONDON SW1

Flight March 10th 1961
Ad Ref 15247

51

LIGHTNING

Mach 2 all-weather fighter in service with The Royal Air Force

...and built by

BRITISH AIRCRAFT CORPORATION

Aeroplane March 17th 1961
Ad Ref 15214

Flight March 30th 1961
Ad Ref 15222

Flight April 13th 1961
Ad Ref 16100

Aeroplane April 20th 1961
Ad Ref 60872

By our standards
the North magnetic pole
doesn't know where it is

If you were at the bottom of a mine-shaft, or in unsurveyed country on a cloudy day, and you had to find true North with high precision, we could help you. We wouldn't use a magnetic compass, which is not nearly sensitive enough, or the Astronomer Royal, who would insist on having a clear view of the sky. We would use one of our fantastically accurate and sensitive floated Gyroscopes. And the job would be done while you waited, to an accuracy of a few minutes of arc.

This is but one of the several complete systems we are working on, taking as our starting point the Gyroscopes we make in partnership with Minneapolis Honeywell and grafting on to them all the arts and skills of the computer designer and the electronics engineer. And we believe we've only scratched the surface of the capabilities and versatilities of Gyroscopes so accurate that they precess barely a degree per *day*, and so sensitive that they respond to a rate of rotation of one revolution in many *years*.

Have you got a problem of this nature which seems to you impossible?

'ENGLISH ELECTRIC'
INERTIAL GUIDANCE
Instrument Wing · Guided Weapons Division

Flight April 20th 1961
Ad Ref 15230

Flight April 27th 1961
Ad Ref 15228

HAY...

A meadow—of no
military significance

Not far away
a vital military area

...PRESTO!

A convoy arrived.

Thunderbird deployed in
less than an hour

The defence
requirement changed
Thunderbird moves rapidly
to where next needed

A meadow remains

THUNDERBIRD

The standard Army A.A. guided weapon
Completely mobile
Easily assembled and serviced

Being developed with C.W. techniques
to extend low level range and now
in an advanced stage of development.

ENGLISH ELECTRIC AVIATION LIMITED A Company of
BRITISH AIRCRAFT CORPORATION
ONE HUNDRED PALL MALL LONDON SW1

Flight April 27th 1961
Ad Ref 15240

58

BEGINNING OF THE END OF A TANK

The target for this Vigilant round may be hull down and a mile away—or it may be only just out of the picture. In either case the tank will never know what hit it.

It will have been knocked out easily, smoothly and surely, by one man—himself hidden, and secure in the knowledge that no flash or smoke from Vigilant has betrayed his position.

VIGILANT one-man anti-tank weapon

VICKERS ARMSTRONG (AIRCRAFT) LTD WEYBRIDGE SURREY A Company of

BRITISH AIRCRAFT CORPORATION
ONE HUNDRED PALL MALL LONDON SW1

Flight April 27th 1961
Ad Ref 15241

59

Aeroplane May 18th 1961
Ad Ref 15209

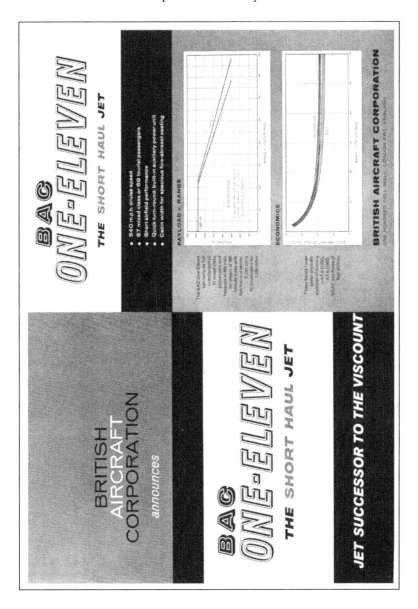

Flight May 18th 1961
Ad Ref 15210

Aeronautics June 1961
Ad Ref 61583

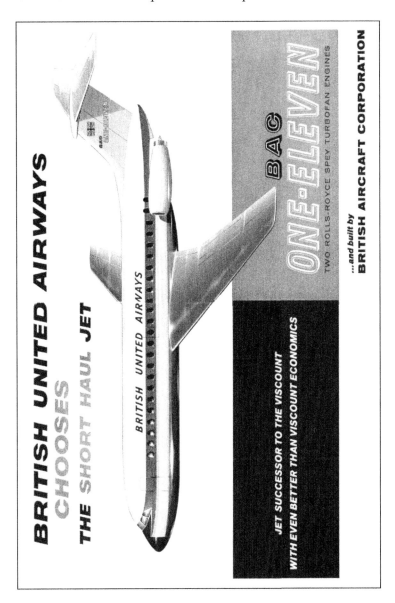

Aeroplane June 8th 1961
Ad Ref 15207

British Aviation Industry Advertisements

By our standards,

bicarbonate of soda

is an abrasive

To produce the fabulously accurate Inertial
Guidance Systems that we manufacture (in partnership with Minneapolis Honeywell) we have had to
build a factory unlike any other you ever saw, and put into it devices of a most unusual kind.
We do our 'sand'-blasting with bicarbonate of soda—and our production-line inspectors use equipment
that other works would be most proud to have in their standards room.
We reckon we've got the most advanced facilities in Europe—but then, we are making the most sensitive
and accurate instruments in the world.
If you have a use for a gyroscope that is so nearly perfect that it only precesses 1/20th of a degree
per hour, and so sensitive that it can find true North, without any outside aid, to within a few minutes
of arc, or if you have a problem involving similar
orders of precision—you should come and talk to us.

'ENGLISH ELECTRIC'
INERTIAL GUIDANCE

INSTRUMENT WING · GUIDED WEAPONS DIVISION · ENGLISH ELECTRIC AVIATION LTD · LUTON AND STEVENAGE

A Company of

BRITISH AIRCRAFT CORPORATION
ONE HUNDRED PALL MALL LONDON SW1

Flight June 8th 1961
Ad Ref 15233

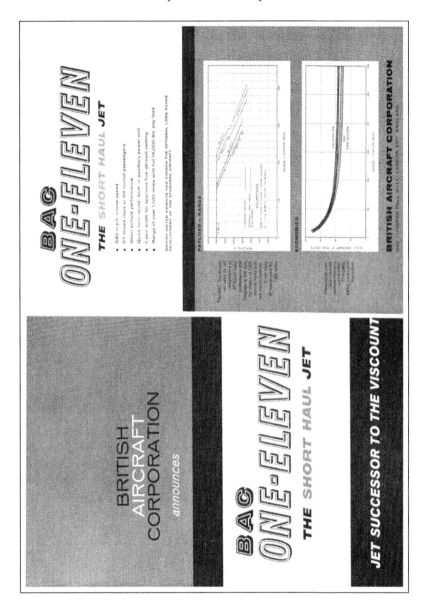

Aeroplane June 22nd 1961
Ad Ref 15208

Aeroplane June 29th 1961
Ad Ref 15236

Aeroplane July 6th 1961
Ad Ref 15235

Aeroplane July 13th 1961
Ad Ref 15206

By our standards, a thousandth of an inch is an agricultural idea

You know about the man who was asked how big a 'thou' was? 'Very, very small' he said. He was asked how many there were in an inch. 'Millions of them' he said.

In this unusual factory of ours—unique in Europe, we suppose—we don't think of a 'thou' as at all small. We have had to train ourselves to take a tolerance of half a tenth in our stride, and to use on our production inspection-line a machine that will measure out-of-roundness of the order of one millionth of an inch.

But then we are in production with instruments the like of which the world has never seen before. We produce (in partnership with Minneapolis Honeywell) Inertial Quality Gyroscopes so accurate that they precess less than half a degree *per day*, so sensitive that you can use them for finding true North to within a few minutes of arc. Small wonder that we do 'sand'-blasting with bicarbonate of soda, and that a speck of dust is a calamity.

'ENGLISH ELECTRIC'
INERTIAL GUIDANCE

INSTRUMENT WING · GUIDED WEAPONS DIVISION · ENGLISH ELECTRIC AVIATION LTD · LUTON AND STEVENAGE

A Company of

BRITISH AIRCRAFT CORPORATION
ONE HUNDRED PALL MALL LONDON SW1

Flight July 27th 1961
Ad Ref 15232

Flight August 10th 1961
Ad Ref 15242

BRITISH UNITED AIRWAYS CHOOSES

THE SHORT HAUL JET

BRITISH UNITED AIRWAYS

BAC ONE-ELEVEN

TWO ROLLS-ROYCE SPEY TURBOFAN ENGINES

JET SUCCESSOR TO THE VISCOUNT
WITH EVEN BETTER THAN VISCOUNT ECONOMICS

- 540 m.p.h. cruise speed
- 57 mixed class or 69 tourist passengers
- Short airfield performance
- Quick turn-round ; built-in auxiliary power unit
- Cabin width for spacious five-abreast seating
- Range of over 1,100 miles with full 14,000 lb payload

BRITISH AIRCRAFT CORPORATION
ONE HUNDRED PALL MALL LONDON SW1 ENGLAND

Aeroplane August 17th 1961
Ad Ref 15205

Aeroplane August 17th 1961
Ad Ref 16099

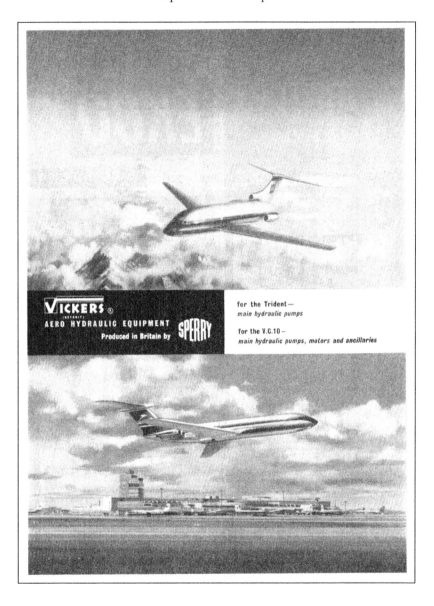

Flight August 17th 1961
Ad Ref 16115

73

Flight August 31st 1961
Ad Ref 15211

LIGHTNING

Chosen for defence by the Royal Air Force

...and built by

BRITISH AIRCRAFT CORPORATION

Flight August 31st 1961
Ad Ref 15215

British Aviation Industry Advertisements

JET PROVOST

Chosen by the Royal Air Force, by Ceylon and by Sudan

...and built by

BRITISH AIRCRAFT CORPORATION

ONE HUNDRED PALL MALL LONDON SW1 ENGLAND

Flight August 31st 1961
Ad Ref 15217

76

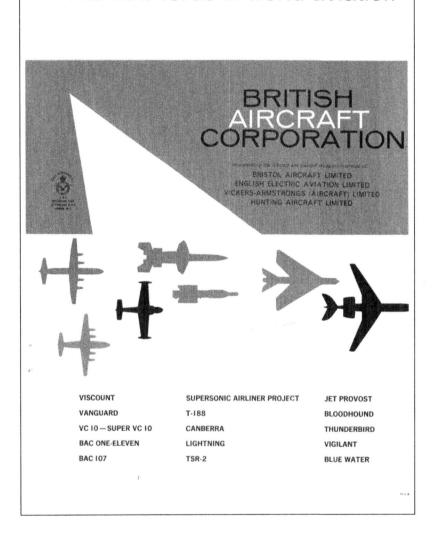

Flight August 31st 1961
Ad Ref 15227

British Aviation Industry Advertisements

...and built by

BLUE WATER

The new surface-to-surface missile
being developed for the British Army

BRITISH AIRCRAFT CORPORATION

Flight August 31st 1961
Ad Ref 15243

Flight August 31st 1961
Ad Ref 15244

Flight August 31st 1961
Ad Ref 15245

PICK ANY SITE...

A field, a clearing in a wood, a road, a hillside — a Thunderbird can roll in on standard service vehicles & without any pre-preparation be deployed in less than one hour.
Mobile, lethal and accurate, Thunderbird is already in service as part of Britain's defence against air attack.
Almost anywhere in the landscape can be an Anti-Aircraft Weapon site when the weapon is Thunderbird.

THUNDERBIRD

ENGLISH ELECTRIC AVIATION LTD STEVENAGE HERTS A Company of

 BRITISH AIRCRAFT CORPORATION

ONE HUNDRED PALL MALL LONDON SW1

Aeronautics September 1961
Ad Ref 61589

British Aviation Industry Advertisements

Flight October 12th 1961
Ad Ref 15246

82

ENGLISH ELECTRIC

AVIATION LIMITED

Require an

Air Traffic Control Officer

Applications are invited from qualified Air Traffic Control Officers to fill a vacancy which has occurred at the Company Airfield, Warton, Lancashire; adjacent to Lytham St. Annes and the modern amenities of Blackpool.

Applicants should be in possession of the M.O.A. Air Traffic Controller's Licence or in a position to qualify with a minimum of delay. A wide knowledge of Air Traffic Control is required coupled with practical experience of control using surveillance/aerodrome radar and associated approach control equipment. Aircrew experience and a knowledge of the control of high-speed jet aircraft would be an advantage.

The appointment is permanent and pensionable and an attractive salary is offered commensurate with age, qualifications and experience.

HEAD
FOR THE
HEIGHTS
with the
new force in
world aviation

Write in confidence to:

J. G. Coop, Room 206/F
English Electric Aviation Limited
Warton Aerodrome, Near Preston
Lancashire

A COMPANY OF
BRITISH AIRCRAFT CORPORATION

Flight October 12th 1961
Ad Ref 15493

83

Flight October 19th 1961
Ad Ref 15229

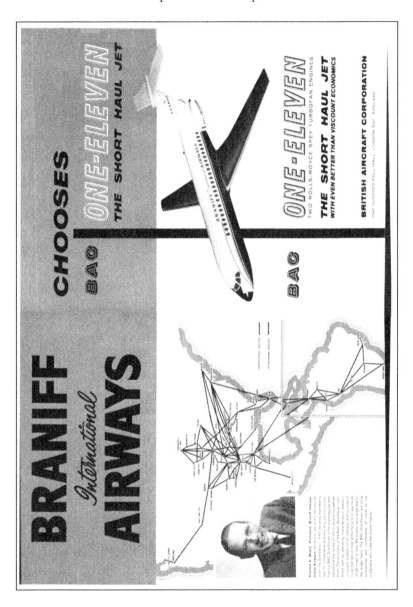

Aeroplane October 26th 1961
Ad Ref 60873

A SINGLE VIGILANT DOES THE WORK OF THREE OF ITS NEXT BEST COMPETITORS

ON OPERATIONS
Vigilant's proven record shows a missile reliability of over 95%, and a 90% record of hits on vulnerable target areas. This is at least twice as good as the record of any comparable infantry anti-tank guided weapon.

IN INITIAL TRAINING
Vigilant's easy-to-learn velocity guidance control cuts training requirements to 5 hours simulator experience plus the firing of only 2 live rounds—at least a 3 to 1 advantage to Vigilant over any other comparable weapon.

IN REFRESHER TRAINING
Only 1 or at most 2 live round firings are needed—another 3 to 1 advantage to Vigilant.

Thus in terms of battlefield effectiveness, Vigilant costs less than any comparable weapon.

VIGILANT
ONE-MAN INFANTRY/PARATROOPER
ANTI-TANK WEAPON

VICKERS-ARMSTRONGS (AIRCRAFT) LTD. WEYBRIDGE, SURREY. A Company of

BRITISH AIRCRAFT CORPORATION
ONE HUNDRED PALL MALL LONDON SW1

Aeroplane November 2nd 1961
Ad Ref 15237

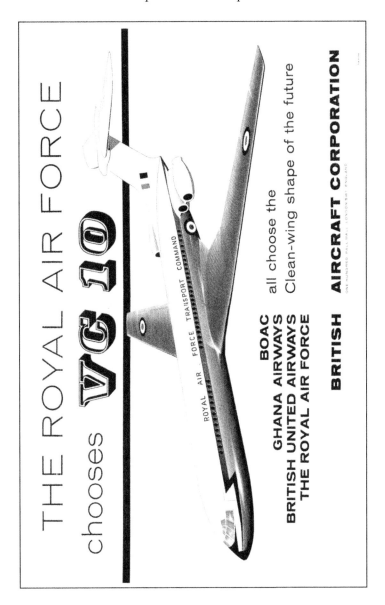

Aeroplane November 9th 1961
Ad Ref 60874

Aeroplane November 23rd 1961
Ad Ref 60875

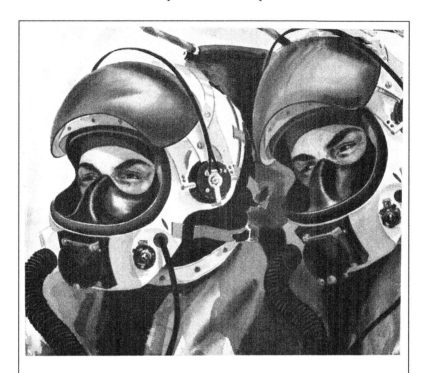

Pilots for the Mach 2 era
are operationally trained
with twin-engined safety in the

IN PRODUCTION FOR THE ROYAL AIR FORCE

ONE HUNDRED PALL MALL   LONDON W1   ENGLAND

Aeroplane December 7th 1961
Ad Ref 15212

Aeroplane December 7th 1961
Ad Ref 15216

Aeroplane December 14th 1961
Ad Ref 15234

Aeronautics January 1962
Ad Ref 61591

Flight January 18th 1962
Ad Ref 39702

Flight January 25th 1962
Ad Ref 51213

Flight February 15th 1962
Ad Ref 51214

Flight March 8th 1962
Ad Ref 39704

Flight March 22nd 1962
Ad Ref 51215

Air Pictorial April 1962
Ad Ref 4140

Flight May 24th 1962
Ad Ref 39707

Flight June 7th 1962
Ad Ref 51212

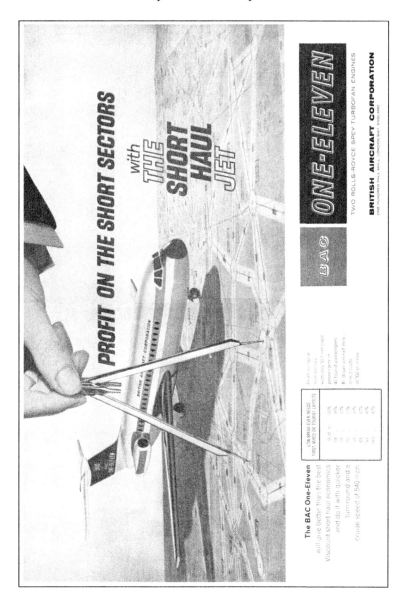

Flight June 28th 1962
Ad Ref 39703

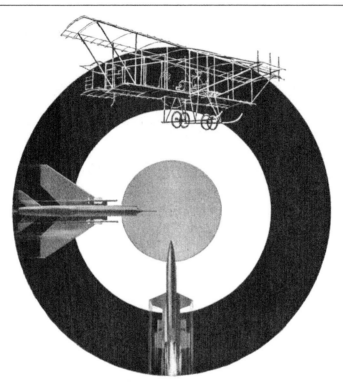

FIFTY OUT OF FIFTY

Since 1912 the member companies of British Aircraft Corporation
have been providing aircraft and weapons for Britain's air defence. It was
with these weapons and aircraft that the men of the
Royal Flying Corps—later the Royal Air Force—made such vital contributions
in two world wars and have maintained security ever since.
British Aircraft Corporation salutes the Royal Air Force and looks
forward to providing its weapons and wings of the future.

BRITISH AIRCRAFT CORPORATION

Air Pictorial August 1962
Ad Ref 4161

Flight August 16th 1962
Ad Ref 39701

Aeroplane September 6th 1962
Ad Ref 60900

Flight September 27th 1962
Ad Ref 39706

Solo jet after only 11 hours

Jet Provost for all-through jet training

BRISTOL SIDDELEY VIPER TURBOJET

That's no record — it's average with the Jet Provost. Because it's a docile plane — easy to fly and easy to land — it safely takes the pupil straight off the ground right into the techniques of jet flying. And he carries on, gaining experience in the same machine until he's ready for advanced training.

The Jet Provost is the only trainer designed from the start for all-through jet training. It produces better pilots more quickly and at far less expense.

The Jet Provost is designed and engineered for easy servicing. It has the lowest labour costs per flying hour of any trainer in the world.

HUNTING AIRCRAFT LTD LUTON AIRPORT BEDFORDSHIRE A Company of

BRITISH AIRCRAFT CORPORATION

ONE HUNDRED PALL MALL LONDON SW1

Air Pictorial October 1962
Ad Ref 4177

Flight October 4th 1962
Ad Ref 39705

Aeroplane October 11th 1962
Ad Ref 39696

Flight October 11th 1962
Ad Ref 51211

109

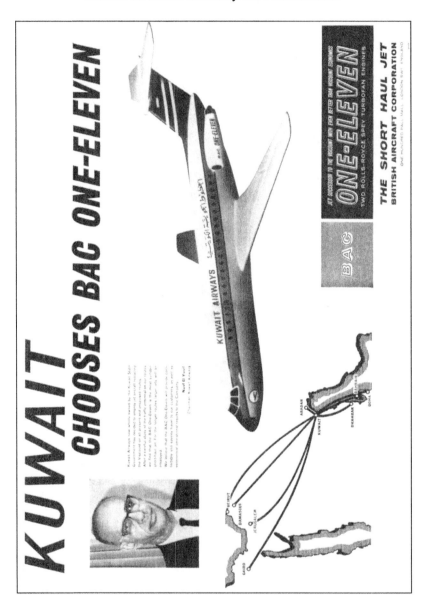

Aeroplane October 25th 1962
Ad Ref 39700

Aeroplane November 22nd 1962
Ad Ref 39699

Aeroplane November 29th 1962
Ad Ref 39695

TSR2 UNDER CONSTRUCTION

Now on the production line, TSR-2 is being built to an advanced requirement which will result in delivery to the Royal Air Force of the world's most flexible tactical strike reconnaissance weapon system.

Cruise at mach 2 plus, operation from short and primitive airfields, extreme low altitude capability, and high accuracy reconnaissance and weapon delivery under blind conditions are a few of the features which give the TSR-2 the degree of freedom required to meet the needs of the Royal Air Force at home and overseas.

TACTICAL · STRIKE · RECONNAISSANCE

Powered by Bristol Siddeley **Olympus** *Turbo-jets*

BRITISH AIRCRAFT CORPORATION
ONE HUNDRED PALL MALL LONDON SW1 ENGLAND

Air Pictorial December 1962
Ad Ref 4182

Aeroplane December 6th 1962
Ad Ref 39698

BRISTOL/FERRANTI

BLOODHOUND

chosen for defence by the United Kingdom,
Australia, Sweden and Switzerland

BRITISH AIRCRAFT CORPORATION

ONE HUNDRED PALL MALL LONDON SW1 ENGLAND

Flight December 6th 1962
Ad Ref 39708

115

Aeroplane January 3rd 1963
Ad Ref 39856

Flight January 24th 1963
Ad Ref 39857

Flight February 7th 1963
Ad Ref 39869

Flight March 7th 1963
Ad Ref 39858

Flight March 21st 1963
Ad Ref 39859

Flight April 25th 1963
Ad Ref 39860

Aeroplane May 16th 1963
Ad Ref 39861

Flight June 6th 1963
Ad Ref 39862

Flight June 20th 1963
Ad Ref 39867

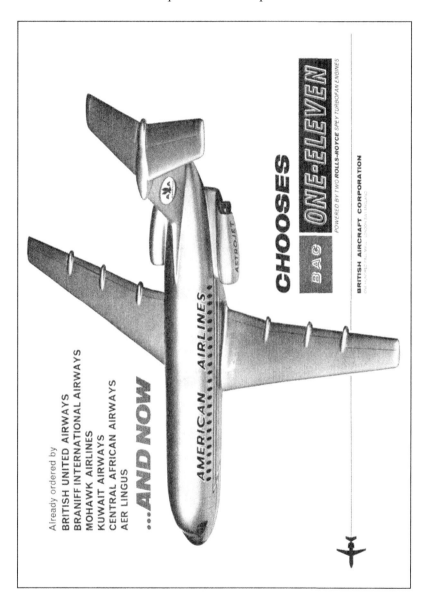

Flight August 29th 1963
Ad Ref 39863

Flight September 26th 1963
Ad Ref 39864

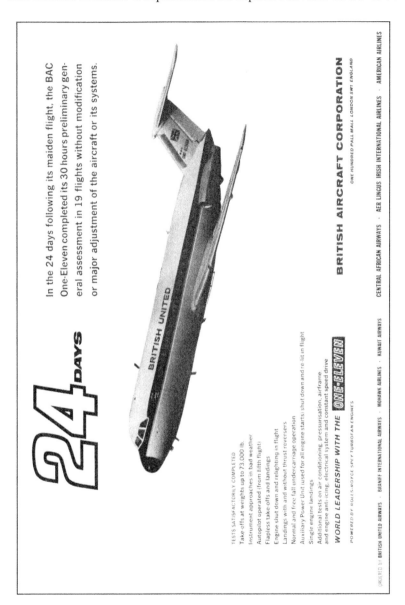

Flight October 10th 1963
Ad Ref 39865

Flight November 14th 1963
Ad Ref 39868

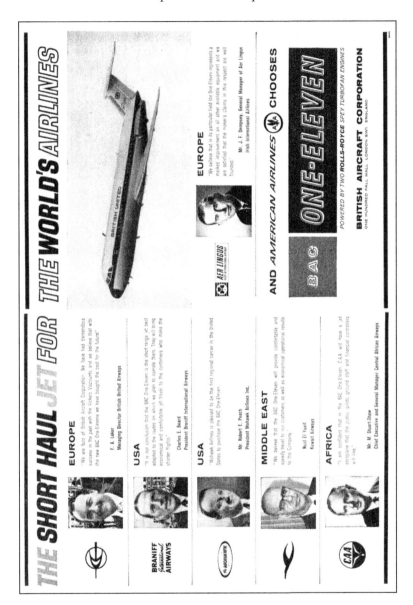

Flight November 28th 1963
Ad Ref 39866

129

TSR2 is capable of modern reconnaissance or of the pin point delivery of any kind of weapon. It is designed to operate at very high speed under the radar screen in all weathers, and has a high degree of invulnerability against any known defence. Its STOL capability frees it from large prepared bases and its long range gives it a flexibility hitherto unattained by any other aircraft. TSR2, which is now on the production line, will augment the operational power of the Royal Air Force in a wide range of roles.

TACTICAL · STRIKE · RECONNAISSANCE

Powered by Bristol Siddeley **Olympus** *Turbo-jets*

BRITISH AIRCRAFT CORPORATION ONE HUNDRED PALL MALL LONDON SW1

Air Pictorial December 1963
Ad Ref 4226

Aeroplane December 19th 1963
Ad Ref 60943

British Aviation Industry Advertisements

ON SCHEDULE

BAC ONE-ELEVENS are in full production for service in 1964

Sixty BAC ONE-ELEVENS are already on order—over half of them for United States operators.

WORLD LEADERSHIP WITH THE

ONE-ELEVEN

POWERED BY TWO ROLLS-ROYCE SPEY TURBOFAN ENGINES

BRITISH AIRCRAFT CORPORATION
ONE HUNDRED PALL MALL LONDON SW1 ENGLAND

ORDERED BY
BRITISH UNITED AIRWAYS · BRANIFF INTERNATIONAL AIRWAYS · MOHAWK AIRLINES · KUWAIT AIRWAYS
CENTRAL AFRICAN AIRWAYS · AER LINGUS IRISH INTERNATIONAL AIRLINES · AMERICAN AIRLINES

Flight January 16th 1964
Ad Ref 40102

132

Aeroplane January 23rd 1964
Ad Ref 52649

Flight February 13th 1964
Ad Ref 40101

Flight March 5th 1964
Ad Ref 40105

Aeroplane March 26th 1964
Ad Ref 52651

Air Pictorial April 1964
Ad Ref 4863

137

Flight April 2nd 1964
Ad Ref 40098

Aeroplane April 23rd 1964
Ad Ref 52650

AIR FORCES
have now chosen the
Jet Provost

BRISTOL SIDDELEY VIPER TURBOJET

The versatile Jet Provost, with its docile low-speed handling qualities, enables pilots without previous flying experience to fly solo after an average of only 11 hours dual—yet its relatively high performance makes it equally suitable for more advanced applied training exercises and tactical support roles.

The Jet Provost is already in service with the Royal Air Force and with the Air Forces of Ceylon, Sudan, Kuwait, Venezuela and has been ordered by Iraq.

BRITISH AIRCRAFT CORPORATION

ONE HUNDRED PALL MALL LONDON SW1 ENGLAND

Flight April 23rd 1964
Ad Ref 40096

THE SHORT HAUL JET IN FULL PRODUCTION

The BAC One-Eleven is in full production
and two-thirds of the orders to date are
for United States operators.

ORDERED BY
BRITISH UNITED AIRWAYS · BRANIFF INTERNATIONAL
AIRWAYS · MOHAWK AIRLINES · KUWAIT AIRWAYS
CENTRAL AFRICAN AIRWAYS · AER LINGUS IRISH
INTERNATIONAL AIRLINES · AMERICAN AIRLINES

WORLD LEADERSHIP WITH THE

POWERED BY TWO **ROLLS-ROYCE** SPEY TURBOFAN ENGINES
BRITISH AIRCRAFT CORPORATION
ONE HUNDRED PALL MALL LONDON SW1 ENGLAND

Flight April 23rd 1964
Ad Ref 40099

141

Aeroplane April 30th 1964
Ad Ref 52653

Air Pictorial May 1964
Ad Ref 4855

143

Flight June 18th 1964
Ad Ref 40104

Aeroplane June 25th 1964
Ad Ref 52652

Flight July 9th 1964
Ad Ref 40097

The British Aircraft Corporation Aerospace Adverts 1960-1977

Flight July 30th 1964
Ad Ref 40103

147

THE PASSENGERS
ARE NOTICING
THE DIFFERENCE

BRITISH AIRCRAFT CORPORATION
ONE HUNDRED PALL MALL LONDON SW1 ENGLAND

Air Pictorial August 1964
Ad Ref 4838

148

Another first ...

'ENGLISH ELECTRIC', pioneers of constant frequency generating systems, have been chosen to supply the ENGLISH ELECTRIC/SUNDSTRAND 60 A.G.D. constant speed drives for the BAC/SUD supersonic airliner.

Concord

Fly with 'ENGLISH ELECTRIC'

STANDS 314 & 315 S.B.A.C. EXHIBITION
FARNBOROUGH. September 7th—13th

AIRCRAFT EQUIPMENT DIVISION
PHOENIX WORKS · BRADFORD
YORKSHIRE · Tel: Bradford 65221

aircraft equipment

The English Electric Company Limited, English Electric House, Strand, London, W.C.2.

Flight September 3rd 1964
Ad Ref 40135

Flight September 10th 1964
Ad Ref 40106

The British Aircraft Corporation Aerospace Adverts 1960-1977

Aeroplane September 17th 1964
Ad Ref 52648

JET TRAINING

400 in service The Royal Air Force chose the jet Provost only after the closest operational and technical evaluation lasting 2 years. Now 6 air forces are using more than 400 Jet Provosts to train their pilots. Present developments ensure continued production.

Solo after 11 hours Docile handling characteristics allow pilots without previous experience to fly solo after an average of only 11 hours dual. Yet performance is more than adequate for the full 160 hour R.A.F. basic training syllabus to be carried out in the same aircraft, including applied flying exercises at high altitudes.

Armament As well as flying training, the Jet Provost is suitable for weapons training and as a tactical strike aircraft in remote areas using airfields denied to more advanced strike aircraft.

Experience The Jet Provost follows two previous R.A.F. basic trainers from the same stable, and total production of all these types so far amounts to more than 1,400 aircraft.

JET PROVOST
BRISTOL SIDDELEY VIPER TURBOJET

BRITISH AIRCRAFT CORPORATION
ONE HUNDRED PALL MALL LONDON SW1 ENGLAND

Air Pictorial October 1964
Ad Ref 4824

152

Flight October 1st 1964
Ad Ref 40108

153

The magnificent VC10

Tributes to the VC10 have now been pouring in from passengers, aviation and travel writers for several months. BOAC describes passenger reaction as "Ecstatic . . without precedent". The international Press have used phrases like "Quietest and most comfortable airliner in the world" — "Dramatic passenger appeal" — "The most admirable jet in existence". An outside test pilot has said, "The nicest transport plane we have ever flown". The passengers have flocked to the aeroplane on all the routes — many preferring to be wait-listed on the VC10 rather than travel in other aircraft. The average load factor on the South African services is 80°₀ on the East African routes, 77°₀. During the period May–August, on the West African routes, it rose from 42°₀ to 75°₀ and to 67°₀ in the Middle East. At the same time the engineering record of the VC10 has been remarkable. An average of 8 hours a day per aircraft in the air ever since introduction with exceptionally low en route technical delays. This record has been described by Mr. Charles Abell, BOAC's Chief Engineer, as "an achievement that few airliners — let alone a new type of airliner—has ever achieved before". For passenger and pilot appeal, rugged reliability, superb engineering and competitive impact the VC10 stands alone.

The Magnificent VC10 *Powered by four Rolls-Royce Conway Engines*

BRITISH AIRCRAFT CORPORATION

ONE HUNDRED PALL MALL LONDON SW1 ENGLAND

Flight November 26th 1964
Ad Ref 40107

PAL LEADS IN ORIENT

ONE-ELEVEN IS ASIA'S FIRST SHORT-HAUL JET

Philippine Air Lines has set the pace for the Orient by choosing the BAC One-Eleven, the world's finest short-haul jet.
When deliveries begin next year, PAL will introduce the Orient's first domestic jet services. PAL's decision is further confirmation that the One-Eleven is, in the judgment of the world's leading short-haul operators, the most efficient and most economical airliner in its field.

A total of 80 One-Elevens is now on order or on option for: British United Airways · Braniff International Airways · Mohawk Airlines · Kuwait Airways · Central African Airways · Aer Lingus Irish International Airlines · American Airlines · Philippine Air Lines · plus four for business transport use.

World leadership with the

POWERED BY TWO **ROLLS-ROYCE** SPEY TURBOFAN ENGINES

BRITISH AIRCRAFT CORPORATION ONE HUNDRED PALL MALL LONDON SW1 ENGLAND

Flight December 3rd 1964
Ad Ref 40100

155

JET TRAINING

400 in service The Royal Air Force chose the jet Provost only after the closest operational and technical evaluation lasting 2 years. Now 6 air forces are using more than 400 Jet Provosts to train their pilots. Present developments ensure continued production.

Solo after 11 hours Docile handling characteristics allow pilots without previous experience to fly solo after an average of only 11 hours dual. Yet performance is more than adequate for the full 160 hour R.A.F. basic training syllabus to be carried out in the same aircraft, including applied flying exercises at high altitudes.

Armament As well as flying training, the Jet Provost is suitable for weapons training and as a tactical strike aircraft in remote areas using airfields denied to more advanced strike aircraft.

Experience The Jet Provost follows two previous R.A.F. basic trainers from the same stable, and total production of all these types so far amounts to more than 1,400 aircraft.

JET PROVOST

BRISTOL SIDDELEY VIPER TURBOJET

AirP60 Jan 1965

BRITISH AIRCRAFT CORPORATION
ONE HUNDRED PALL MALL LONDON SW1 ENGLAND

BHP 158

Air Pictorial January 1965
Ad Ref 4589

A NEW JET TRAINER

British Aircraft Corporation has been awarded a contract to develop for the Royal Air Force a pressurised jet trainer, the BAC 145, to be known in the RAF as the Jet Provost T Mk 5.

Design of the BAC 145 is backed by the experience already gained in over 300,000 Jet Provost flying hours and in producing already more than 450 Jet Provosts for the RAF and five overseas Air Forces. Jet Provost flight experience, supplemented by exhaustive fatigue research carried out during actual flying training programmes, enables an airframe life of 15 years, assuming normal utilisation, to be confidently forecast for the BAC 145. Versatile, and as reliable as the Jet Provost, it retains the well-proven Bristol Siddeley Viper engine and, with its pressurised cockpit will allow protracted training exercises to be carried out at high altitude in safety and comfort thus widening still more the scope of the syllabus that can be undertaken by a single aircraft type.

BRITISH AIRCRAFT CORPORATION

100 PALL MALL LONDON SW1 ENGLAND

BHF 11

Flight January 14th 1965
Ad Ref 40324

Aeroplane January 21st 1965
Ad Ref 60945

BAC

ONE-ELEVEN

The test programme for the One-Eleven is the most comprehensive ever devised for an airliner.
All 14 design loading cases—up to 85% of the ultimate—have been covered in the structural test programme. Static testing of the complete structure has proved substantial reserves of strength above the design requirement. The picture shows the wing sustaining four and a half times a normal steady flight load. In fatigue tests, a specimen fuselage has completed the equivalent of 30,000 flights and a complete wing and fuselage will now complete another 100,000.
Nothing less than this tough testing is enough for the tough operations ahead—and it's one of the reasons why the One-Eleven is the finest short-haul airliner ever built.

The finest short-haul airliner ever built

World leadership with the One-Eleven
POWERED BY TWO **ROLLS-ROYCE** SPEY TURBOFAN ENGINES

ORDERED BY BRITISH UNITED AIRWAYS · BRANIFF INTERNATIONAL AIRWAYS · MOHAWK AIRLINES
KUWAIT AIRWAYS · CENTRAL AFRICAN AIRWAYS · AER LINGUS IRISH INTERNATIONAL AIRLINES
AMERICAN AIRLINES · PHILIPPINE AIR LINES · PLUS FOUR FOR EXECUTIVE FLYING

BA566

BRITISH AIRCRAFT CORPORATION 100 PALL MALL LONDON SW1

Flight February 11th 1965
Ad Ref 40321

159

British Aviation Industry Advertisements

new customer
ORDERS

existing customer
RE-ORDERS

Aloha Airlines,
which has ordered two
BAC One-Elevens
for operation on its
short-journey services
between the Hawaiian Islands,
has become the ninth airline
in the world
and the fourth in the U.S.A.
to order the finest
short-haul airliner ever built.

Mohawk Airlines
of New York, which placed
its first order
for BAC One-Elevens
in July 1962
and increased it
in March 1964,
has now raised it once again
—to a firm order
for seven aircraft,
with an option on a further three.

ONE-ELEVEN

ORDERED BY AER LINGUS—IRISH INTERNATIONAL AIRLINES ☐ ALOHA AIRLINES ☐ AMERICAN AIRLINES ☐ BRANIFF INTERNATIONAL AIRWAYS
BRITISH UNITED AIRWAYS ☐ CENTRAL AFRICAN AIRWAYS ☐ KUWAIT AIRWAYS ☐ MOHAWK AIRLINES ☐ PHILIPPINE AIR LINES

BRITISH AIRCRAFT CORPORATION
100 PALL MALL LONDON SW1

Aeroplane March 25th 1965
Ad Ref 60946

160

Flight April 15th 1965
Ad Ref 40320

161

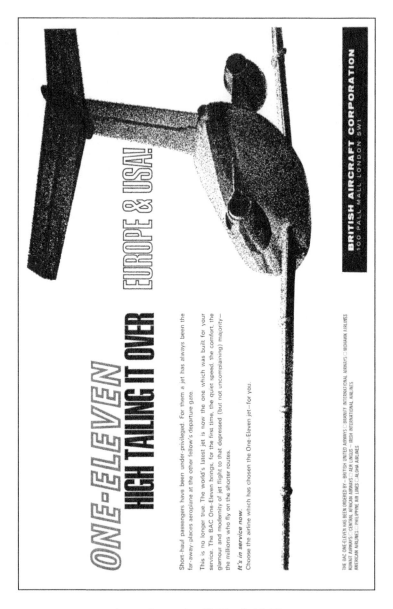

Aeroplane April 22nd 1965
Ad Ref 60947

NEW STANDARDS OF AIR TRAVEL COMFORT
are being pioneered throughout the world by British Aircraft Corporation's two rear-engined jet airliners, the magnificent VC10 intercontinental airliner and the short-haul BAC One-Eleven

BOTH BUILT BY BRITISH AIRCRAFT CORPORATION

100 PALL MALL LONDON SW1

BAC 73

Aeroplane August 5th 1965
Ad Ref 60948

163

Flight October 21st 1965
Ad Ref 40323

Flight November 18th 1965
Ad Ref 40325

Flight November 25th 1965
Ad Ref 40322

British Midland and TACA select the

PROVEN JET

Half the world apart, British Midland Airways in the United Kingdom and TACA International Airlines in Central America have to contend with completely different operating requirements and completely different traffic patterns. Both, however, seek to give their passengers the most modern, most efficient air transport — and both have found their answer in the BAC One-Eleven, the only short-haul jet already profitably proven in revenue-earning service.

ONE-ELEVEN

BRITISH AIRCRAFT CORPORATION

Aeroplane December 16th 1965
Ad Ref 60949

The Australian Government has chosen the One-Eleven

The Australian Government's decision to purchase two BAC One-Elevens for its VIP passenger services underlines the outstanding qualities of the aircraft in the executive role. Possessing a transocean, transcontinental range which gives it a genuine global capability, the One-Eleven is the smallest jet able to offer real "walk-around" comfort on long flights. The design features and engineering strength which have made the One-Eleven the world's finest short-haul airliner might also have been tailor-made for the VIP transport role—the auxiliary power unit and powered airsteps which enable the aircraft to use any airfield without dependence on ground services . . . the exceptional flight-deck vision which takes many of the worries out of small-field operation . . . the ease of maintenance and structural ruggedness . . . the twin-systems reliability . . . the superb air-conditioning and pressurisation system . . . the all-round comfort. But, above all, the BAC One-Eleven possesses the unique advantage of being the only jet executive transport already proven in airline service.

BRITISH AIRCRAFT CORPORATION

100 PALL MALL · LONDON S.W.1

Aeroplane January 13th 1966
Ad Ref 60996

As the spearhead of its
new air defence system,
Saudi Arabia has selected
the Lightning, one of the world's
most advanced combat aircraft.
Continuous development
in squadron service
with the Royal Air Force
has made the latest
production version of this Mach 2
fighter virtually a completely
new weapons system, the equal
of any in service today.
The complementary two-seat trainer,
also chosen by Saudi Arabia,
provides not only an advanced training
facility but an added operational capability

Saudi Arabia selects the
LIGHTNING

BRITISH AIRCRAFT CORPORATION
100 PALL MALL, LONDON S.W.1.

Flight January 27th 1966
Ad Ref 40696

169

To step up its
pilot-training capability
to keep pace with the requirements
of its expanding,
modernised air force,
Saudi Arabia has selected
the pressurised and most powerful version
of the Jet Provost.
Into the development of this
versatile new trainer has gone
the experience gained from the
production of more than
450 Jet Provosts for the
Royal Air Force
and five overseas air forces
and, in particular, the hard,
practical knowledge derived
from over 400,000 flying hours.

Saudi Arabia selects the

Jet Provost

BRITISH AIRCRAFT CORPORATION
100 PALL MALL, LONDON S.W.1.

Flight January 27th 1966
Ad Ref 40699

Air Pictorial April 1966
Ad Ref 4487

British Aviation Industry Advertisements

Flying Review April 1966
Ad Ref 40698

172

THE PROOF
FROM USA ON A BRITISH JET

The American Civil Aeronautics Board in a tribute to the British One-Eleven short-haul jetliner now in service in USA says "It appears that for the first time in aviation history it may be possible to operate aircraft at relatively short stage lengths at operating costs which approach the same cost for longer haul aircraft. This permits an optimistic view of the potential for improved service for our intermediate cities".

The One-Eleven, in service in USA and Europe, is now making nearly 25% clear profit. It is showing operating costs 10% below estimate and maintenance costs averaging 27% below estimate. It has utilisation records up to nearly ten hours a day and proven across-the-board passenger increases on routes to over 60 cities.

ONE-ELEVEN

The BAC One-Eleven is the *only* short-haul jet which can back its claims by proven facts

BUILT BY BRITISH AIRCRAFT CORPORATION

BAS R8a

Flight April 14th 1966
Ad Ref 40690

173

THE PROOF

The One-Eleven is already making nearly 25% clear profit over all operating costs, including overheads.
The One-Eleven with 9 months of service in USA and Europe behind it is being sold on facts and not wishful thinking.
Facts such as:

Maintenance costs have averaged 27% below the estimates on which Braniff International of USA bought the One-Eleven.

Braniff's actual total operating costs are 10% below estimate.

The One-Eleven is breaking even (all costs) on 33 passengers per 245 mile average stage—but actually seats up to 79 passengers.

Braniff's ten aircraft are each averaging nine profit making flights per aircraft per day—and utilisation has already reached 10 hours a day.

Mohawk—another USA customer reports a 35% traffic increase with One-Elevens; British United a 50% increase; Aer Lingus Irish International up to 63%.

ONE-ELEVEN

The BAC One-Eleven is the only short-haul jet which can back its claims by proven facts

BUILT BY BRITISH AIRCRAFT CORPORATION

Aeroplane April 21st 1966
Ad Ref 60997

174

One-Eleven—setting the pace

in the U.S. and Latin America

In scheduled airline operation in the USA and Europe for the past twelve months, the BAC One-Eleven—the only fully service-proven short-haul jet—has set the pace in bringing the speed, comfort and smoothness of jet travel to short/medium-range inter-city routes. Now orders from four leading Latin American airlines—TACA of El Salvador, LACSA of Costa Rica, LANICA of Nicaragua and AEROCONDOR of Colombia—have clearly established the One-Eleven as the jet-age pace-setter in the south of the Continent as well as the north.

BRITISH AIRCRAFT CORPORATION 100 PALL MALL LONDON S.W.1

BAC 106A

Flight May 26th 1966
Ad Ref 40695

175

We are
often asked
what we mean by

the 'pay-off' of short-haul experience and British engineering

What we mean
are figures like these:—

BAC One-Eleven Complete Year of USA Operations on First-Delivery Aircraft

WHEN DELIVERED	REGISTRATION	CARRIER	LANDINGS	HOURS
11 March 1965	N1543	Braniff	4040	2780
6 April 1965	N1544	Braniff	3760	2888
20 April 1965	N1542	Braniff	3790	2925
12 May 1965	N1545	Braniff	4080	3020
15 May 1965	N2111J	Mohawk	3985	2335
Average for first 365 days			**3931**	**2789**

ONE-ELEVEN

Built by BRITISH AIRCRAFT CORPORATION
Powered by Rolls-Royce

Flight June 23rd 1966
Ad Ref 40692

Flight July 7th 1966
Ad Ref 40701

177

Flying Review July 1966
Ad Ref 40702

We are
often asked
what we mean by

the 'pay-off' of short-haul experience and British engineering

What we mean
are figures like these:—

BAC One-Eleven Complete Year of USA Operations on First-Delivery Aircraft

WHEN DELIVERED	REGISTRATION	CARRIER	LANDINGS	HOURS
11 March 1965	N1543	Braniff	4040	2780
6 April 1965	N1544	Braniff	3760	2888
20 April 1965	N1542	Braniff	3790	2925
12 May 1965	N1545	Braniff	4080	3020
15 May 1965	N2111J	Mohawk	3985	2335
Average for first 365 days			3931	2789

ONE-ELEVEN

Built by BRITISH AIRCRAFT CORPORATION
Powered by Rolls-Royce

BRITISH AIRCRAFT CORPORATION
100 PALL MALL LONDON SW1

BAS 113

Flight July 21st 1966
Ad Ref 40694

179

ÜBERRAGENDE ERFOLGE

WELTWEIT FÜHREND MIT DER

ONE-ELEVEN

AUSGERÜSTET MIT ZWEI MANTELSTROMTRIEBWERKEN **ROLLS-ROYCE** SPEY

Schon lange bevor die BAC One-Eleven zu ihrem Erstflug startete, wurden mit diesem naturgroßen Modell des Steuer- und Hydrauliksystems viele One-Eleven-Flugstunden absolviert. Zur Zeit der Indienststellung des Flugzeuges wird der Prüfstand 7000 „Flüge" durchgeführt haben – entsprechend einem zweijährigen Einsatz im Luftverkehr.

Das Erprobungsprogramm der One-Eleven – von dem diese Prüfung nur einen sehr kleinen Teil darstellt – beeindruckte die Ingenieure der Luftverkehrsgesellschaften. Es handelt sich um die gründlichste Erprobung, der ein Kurzstreckenflugzeug jemals unterzogen wurde. Die Aufstellung dieses Programms erfolgte unter Mitwirkung der erfahrensten Fachleute.

Bestellt von

BRITISH UNITED AIRWAYS · BRANIFF INTERNATIONAL AIRWAYS
MOHAWK AIRLINES · KUWAIT AIRWAYS · CENTRAL AFRICAN AIRWAYS
AER LINGUS IRISH INTERNATIONAL AIRLINES · AMERICAN AIRLINES

BRITISH AIRCRAFT CORPORATION
ONE HUNDRED PALL MALL LONDON SW1
Richten Sie alle Anfragen en:
G. H. Waugh, KÖLN RHEIN, Nürnberger Haus, Apostelnstraße 3

Flug Revue International August 1966
Ad Ref 87609

We are
often asked
what we mean by

**the 'pay-off'
of short-haul experience
and British engineering**

What we mean
are figures like these:—

NUMBER OF ONE-ELEVENS IN AIRLINE SERVICE FOR PERIOD EXAMINED	ACHIEVEMENT
Braniff International First service April 25, 1965 *Eleven for 6 month period ended May 11*	11.5 sectors flown per aircraft per day, 980,000 passengers carried 62.8 per cent load factor, 22,591 landings. (Since the beginning of this year, 14 One-Elevens have been in Braniff service)
American Airlines First service March 6, 1966 *Four during April*	Overall load factor averaged over 70 per cent in April
Philippine Airlines First service May 1, 1966 *One*	Sixty-nine hours flying per week scheduled and achieved from outset with passengers load factor exceeding 70 per cent on international flights
Aloha Airlines First service April 29, 1966 *One*	121 revenue flights made in the first 19 days, over 130 mile average sectors plus an additional four hours per day of flight crew training
Mohawk Airlines First service July 15, 1965 *Five*	"Today Mohawk's One-Elevens, fully loaded with sixty-nine passengers, baggage and cargo are turned around at terminal points in ten minutes and are serviced at intermediate passenger points with partial passenger loads on and off, including fuel, in six minutes." *Extract from 1965 Annual Report of Mohawk Airlines Inc.*

ONE-ELEVEN

Built by BRITISH AIRCRAFT CORPORATION Powered by Rolls-Royce

BRITISH AIRCRAFT CORPORATION
100 PALL MALL LONDON SW1

BAS 114

Flight August 25th 1966
Ad Ref 40691

181

BRITISH AIRCRAFT CORPORATION

THE BEST OF EVERYTHING

TRANSPORTS

*CONCORDE — *first supersonic airliner*

VC10 — *long-range subsonic airliner*

BAC ONE-ELEVEN — *short/medium-range jet airliner*

MILITARY AIRCRAFT

*JAGUAR — *supersonic strike/fighter trainer*

*VARIABLE GEOMETRY — *combat aircraft*

LIGHTNING — *interceptor fighter*

BAC 145/167 — *new jet trainer*

GUIDED WEAPONS

ET316 — *low level anti-aircraft defence*

SWINGFIRE — *anti-tank missile*

VIGILANT — *anti-tank missile*

BLOODHOUND — *ground defence*

THUNDERBIRD — *ground defence*   *Anglo/French Joint Projects.

Each and every one of these products is the best of its kind in the world

BRITISH AIRCRAFT CORPORATION
100 PALL MALL LONDON SW1

Air Pictorial September 1966
Ad Ref 4559

182

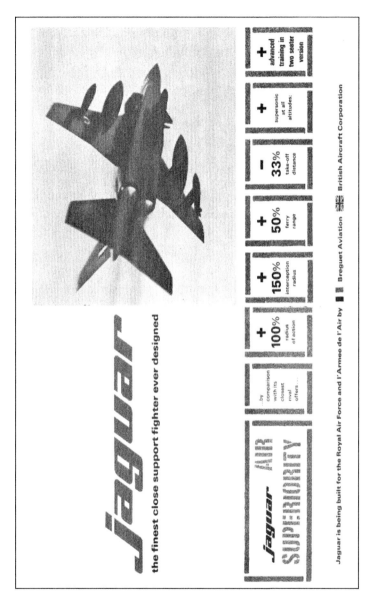

Flying Review October 1966
Ad Ref 40700

We are
often asked
what we mean by

the 'pay-off' of short-haul experience and British engineering

What we mean
are figures like these:—

BAC ONE-ELEVEN—FIRST COMMERCIAL SERVICES—APRIL 1965

ACHIEVEMENT	In the first 16 months of service sixty five One-Elevens delivered. Over 120,000 landings completed.
OPERATED BY	Eight airlines and two business corporations.
SERVING	57 cities in USA (including Hawaii) and a further 52 in Europe, Africa and the Far East.
ACHIEVED FLEET UTILISATION	Up to 14 airline sectors per aircraft per day.
SECTOR DISTANCES	from below 100 miles to over 1,300 miles.
PRODUCTIVITY	First ten One-Elevens delivered to USA each averaged 4,020 landings in their first 365 days of service.
ACHIEVED COSTS IN USA OPERATION	Aircraft mile costs—lowest of any jet in service. Seat mile costs and maintenance costs—lower than 40-50 seat, twin engined piston and prop-jet airliners.

ONE-ELEVEN

Built by BRITISH AIRCRAFT CORPORATION Powered by Rolls-Royce

BRITISH AIRCRAFT CORPORATION
100 PALL MALL LONDON SW1

BAS 115

Flight October 20th 1966
Ad Ref 40693

184

INTERCEPTOR SUPREME

The latest production version of the incomparable Lightning fighter—the Royal Air Force's interceptor supreme—is soon also to join the Royal Saudi Air Force.

Today's Lightning—developed against a background of continuous RAF service—is virtually a completely new weapons system and is the equal of any aircraft in the world. A continuous development programme is exploiting the immense potential of the Lightning basic design and the great and growing volume of service experience.

LIGHTNING

BRITISH AIRCRAFT CORPORATION

100 PALL MALL LONDON SW1

Flying Review December 1966
Ad Ref 40697

185

DISTINGUISHED BREEDING

Breeding and background will always tell. The BAC 167 is a new trainer-strike jet with half a million jet-trainer flying hours in its ancestry and with 1,400 military training aircraft in its family tree. It inherits its ideal instructor-pupil lay-out and its pressure cabin from the BAC 145, now being developed for the Royal Air Force, while its fighter-crisp handling makes it the perfect stablemate for its supersonic relative, the incomparable Lightning.

The BAC 167, with the latest and most powerful Bristol Siddeley Viper engine, is the operational trainer which is also truly operational. It can be used for weapon training and for precision ground attack.

The BAC 167's blend of power and performance with strength and reliability makes it the most thoroughbred of all trainer-strike aircraft.

Now entering production for the Royal Saudi Air Force

BRITISH AIRCRAFT CORPORATION 100 PALL MALL LONDON S.W.1

Interavia December 1966
Ad Ref 76932

186

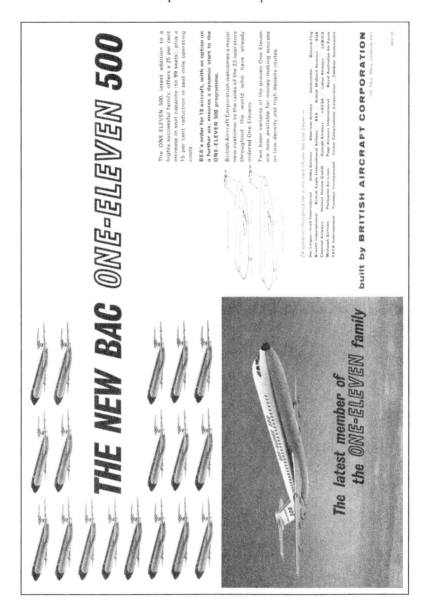

Flight January 19th 1967
Ad Ref 40969

187

British Aviation Industry Advertisements

Flying Review March 1967
Ad Ref 40971

it has been proved

that 15 passengers cover the direct operating costs of a BAC One-Eleven on a 260 mile stage. There is then room for 64 more passengers to cover the overheads and to produce the profit.

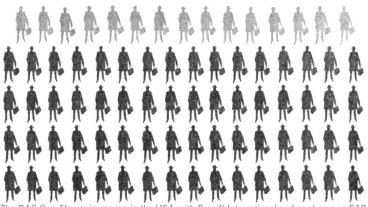

The BAC One-Eleven, in service in the USA with Braniff International and as shown in CAB returns over a year, has cost $1.09 per aircraft mile on an average stage length of 260 statute miles. The average fare revenue was 7.4 cents per passenger mile. *Simple arithmetic shows that 14.7 passengers pay the DOC's.*

BAC ONE-ELEVEN

The most economic short-haul jet in its class in the world

25 operators throughout the world have chosen the One-Eleven :-
Aer Lingus—Irish International ☐ Aerocondor ☐ Aloha Airlines ☐ American Airlines ☐ Autair International Airways ☐ Bavaria Flug Braniff International ☐ British Eagle International Airlines ☐ British European Airways ☐ British Midland Airways ☐ BUA ☐ Channel Airways Helmut Horten GmbH ☐ Kuwait Airways ☐ LACSA ☐ Laker Airways ☐ LANICA ☐ Mohawk Airlines ☐ Philippine Air Lines ☐ Page Airways International Royal Australian Air Force ☐ TACA International ☐ Tenneco Incorporated ☐ Victor Comptometer Corporation ☐ Zambian Government

built by BRITISH AIRCRAFT CORPORATION

BAS 130   100 PALL MALL LONDON SW1

Flight April 13th 1967
Ad Ref 40966

189

Flight May 25th 1967
Ad Ref 40970

Air Pictorial June 1967
Ad Ref 4388

The first all-British satellite was successfully placed in orbit on May 5th and marks a significant stage in Britain's space programme. British Aircraft Corporation, through their collaboration with leading American space manufacturers, their work on U.K.3, the Skylark Sounding Rocket, HEOS Satellite and other space research projects, are making a major contribution to Britain's progress in space technology.

Experiments devised by Universities of Birmingham, Sheffield and Manchester, the Meteorological Office, Radio and Research Station.
Main contractors: British Aircraft Corporation Limited and General Electric Company Limited.
Organisation teams include Science Research Council, Ministry of Aviation and Royal Aircraft Establishment. British Aircraft Corporation were responsible for programme co-ordination, structures, testing, integration and ground check-out equipment.

ALL BRITISH

BRITISH AIRCRAFT CORPORATION
Guided Weapons Division · Stevenage & Bristol · England

Flight July 27th 1967
Ad Ref 40973

192

Flight August 10th 1967
Ad Ref 40967

Air Pictorial September 1967
Ad Ref 4412

Flight September 7th 1967
Ad Ref 40972

British Aviation Industry Advertisements

THE SKY IS
NOT
THE LIMIT

Extending the frontiers of knowledge is the everyday business of the aerospace industry. New design concepts, new manufacturing techniques, new materials must constantly be developed to meet the unceasing demand for increased capability and higher performance. The design and engineering teams of British Aircraft Corporation bring together the knowledge and experience accumulated in over 50 years of continuous technical advance in, first, military and commercial aviation and, more recently, in defence weapon systems and space research equipment. Their skill and ability, backed by massive technical facilities, not only ensure that Britain remains a leader in aerospace but also provides the driving force for technological development over a far wider industrial field.
For British Aircraft Corporation, even the sky is not the limit.

CONCORDE · BAC ONE-ELEVEN · VC10 · VG · JAGUAR · LIGHTNING · BAC 145/167 · JET PROVOST · UK3
RAPIER · BLOODHOUND · THUNDERBIRD · SWINGFIRE · VIGILANT · INDUSTRIAL & PLASTICS PRODUCTS

BRITISH AIRCRAFT CORPORATION

ONE HUNDRED PALL MALL LONDON SW1   BAC 86

Air Pictorial November 1967
Ad Ref 4421

196

An exciting, expanding world of advanced technology

BRITISH AIRCRAFT CORPORATION
Guided Weapons Division Stevenage and Bristol England

Air Pictorial December 1967
Ad Ref 4424

Flight December 14th 1967
Ad Ref 40968

Flight January 18th 1968
Ad Ref 41286

199

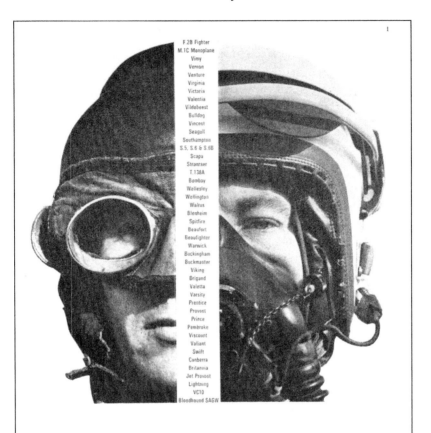

F.2B Fighter
M.1C Monoplane
Vimy
Vernon
Venture
Virginia
Victoria
Valentia
Vildebeest
Bulldog
Vincent
Seagull
Southampton
S.5, S.6 & S.6B
Scapa
Stranraer
T.138A
Bombay
Wellesley
Wellington
Walrus
Blenheim
Spitfire
Beaufort
Beaufighter
Warwick
Buckingham
Buckmaster
Viking
Brigand
Valetta
Varsity
Prentice
Provost
Prince
Pembroke
Viscount
Valiant
Swift
Canberra
Britannia
Jet Provost
Lightning
VC10
Bloodhound SAGW

From the formation of the Royal Air Force on April 1st, 1918, to the present day, there has never been a time when RAF roundels were not proudly worn by aircraft designed and manufactured by the companies of

BRITISH AIRCRAFT CORPORATION
Since they laid the foundation of British strength in the air with the Boxkite of 1910 and the Gun-Bus of 1913, these companies have built for the Royal Flying Corps and Royal Air Force over 75,000 aircraft.

Flight March 28th 1968
Ad Ref 41289

We helped to write this American Airlines success story!

"Seems like only yesterday that American's newest fleet went into service. Yet the company's 30 BAC One-Elevens have already chalked up remarkable achievements in carrying more than 3½ million passengers". So said American Airlines' employee magazine, ASTROJET, and it went on to explain just what those achievements were in the following words.

"American's first British-built BAC One-Eleven flew into service in March of last year. The final plane – completing the fleet at 30 aircraft – went on-line earlier this year. The time span is only a matter of months, yet the fleet has already charted a billion revenue passenger miles – a record attesting not only to the proficiency of AA flight crews and maintenance men, but also to the ability of the plane itself.

"It was with tremendous success that the short-haul workhorse was used to launch American's Jet Express services in the East. Statistics tell the story. In January of this year, American carried 5,000 passengers between New York and Boston for a paltry 3% of this huge market. Since inauguration of the Jet Express, using the BAC One-Eleven, that share has risen sharply to 24% of the Boston-LGA/JFK market. American is now carrying more than 35,000 passengers a month between the two cities.

"A similar story can be told for the New York-Washington Jet Express. American had 19% of the market in June when it carried about 29,000 passengers. When Jet Express was introduced the market penetration rose to 27% for a passenger count of 37,000 in August between LGA/JFK and Washington.

"Not only has the Astrojet 400 effectively penetrated new markets, but it has done so against the formidable competition of larger jets. Take the Boston-Washington nonstop as an example. During June,

American offered 13 Astrojet 400 flights (plus one 727) daily between the two cities. This was in the face of high density competition offered by Northeast and Eastern which between them scheduled nineteen 727 flights daily (plus six Electra flights). Despite this, the load factor for American's BAC One-Elevens on this route during June was a superb 86%. In May it was 81%, in July 82%, and in August 84% – undeniable evidence of the aircraft's ability to compete.

"How has American's newest plane fared on dependability? Right up with the best of the other equipment, and better in many instances. During September, 81.9% of all BAC One-Eleven departures were within five minutes of scheduled time – tops for any fleet in the system.

"Measured in terms of physical performance the BAC One-Eleven fares equally as well. Despite the relative inexperience in maintenance, the Astrojet 400 fleet has consistently ranked near the top in fewest number of delays because of mechanical troubles. Indeed the mechanics at the LaGuardia fleet base station say that the 'Baccala,' as they affectionately call her, is a 'real fine' plane to maintain due mainly to its low-slung accessibility."

BAC ONE-ELEVEN
In service with and on order for 30 operators worldwide

Flight April 11th 1968
Ad Ref 41281

201

Flight May 9th 1968
Ad Ref 41291

202

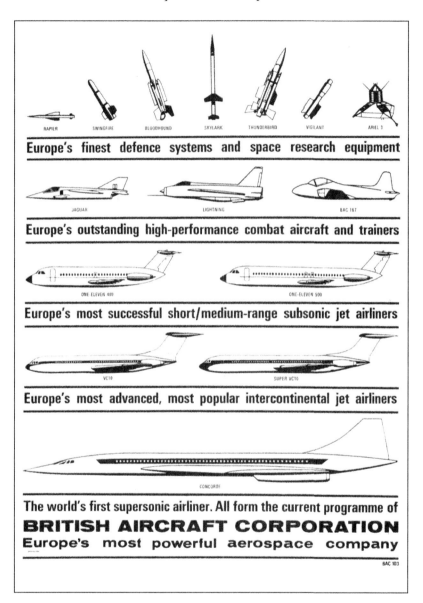

Europe's finest defence systems and space research equipment

Europe's outstanding high-performance combat aircraft and trainers

Europe's most successful short/medium-range subsonic jet airliners

Europe's most advanced, most popular intercontinental jet airliners

The world's first supersonic airliner. All form the current programme of

BRITISH AIRCRAFT CORPORATION
Europe's most powerful aerospace company

Air Pictorial June 1968
Ad Ref 4732

Flight June 27th 1968
Ad Ref 41282

Flight July 4th 1968
Ad Ref 41283

205

BRITISH AIRCRAFT CORPORATION
the most powerful aerospace
company in Europe

BAC aircraft and weapons systems have been chosen by over half of all the countries in the world.

Rapier is the world's finest and latest mobile tactical low level AA missile system. It has already destroyed low flying ground attack jet aircraft (above) and has hit a towed low level "drainpipe" target, measuring 19 cm x 2.13 m, at 3 kms range.

BRITISH AIRCRAFT CORPORATION
100 PALL MALL LONDON SW1

BAC 204

Flight July 18th 1968
Ad Ref 41290

The British Aircraft Corporation Aerospace Adverts 1960-1977

Flight August 15th 1968
Ad Ref 41285

207

British Aviation Industry Advertisements

Flying Review September 1968
Ad Ref 41288

208

Aeroplane September 11th 1968
Ad Ref 61057

BRITISH AIRCRAFT CORPORATION
the most powerful aerospace
company in Europe

BAC aircraft and weapons systems have been chosen
by over half of all the countries in the world.

The Lightning, which in RAF service has
proved itself the world's finest interceptor, has now been
given a formidable ground attack capability and is entering
service in Saudi Arabia and Kuwait. Dual capability – combining the roles of trainer and versatile ground attack
weapon – also characterises the BAC 167,
latest in a line of jet trainers operated or
ordered by eleven air forces.

BRITISH AIRCRAFT CORPORATION
100 PALL MALL LONDON SW1

Circle No. 11 on Reader Service Coupon   BAC201

Flying Review October 1968
Ad Ref 41292

210

Flight October 24th 1968
Ad Ref 41287

Flight November 21st 1968
Ad Ref 41284

Air Pictorial January 1969
Ad Ref 4906

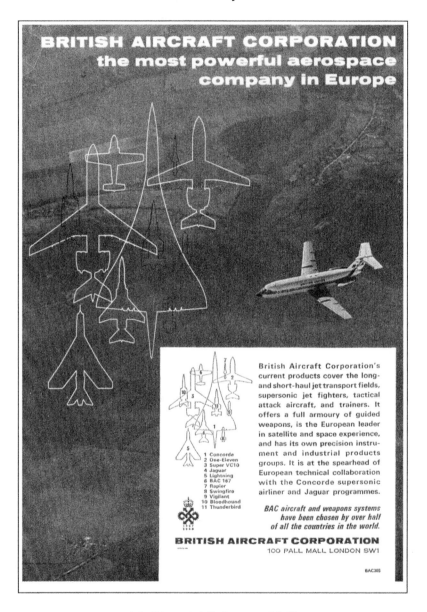

Air Pictorial February 1969
Ad Ref 4896

Interavia March 1969
Ad Ref 82209

215

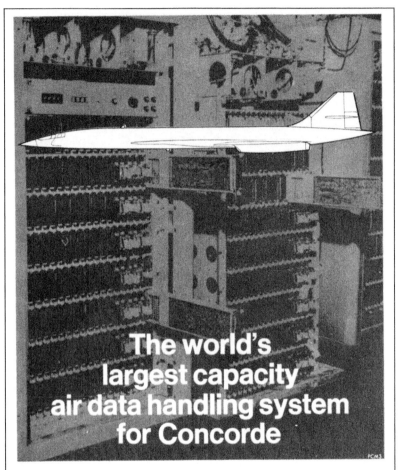

The first two air data handling systems for Concorde's flight test programme were designed and manufactured by the Space and Instrumentation Group of British Aircraft Corporation. Capable of the continuous sampling, digitising and recording of 2600 parameters at rates of up to 25 samples per second, they are the world's largest capacity flight recording systems. Here is yet another 'first' for BAC, Europe's most powerful aerospace company.

BRITISH AIRCRAFT CORPORATION

Space and Instrumentation Group.
Bristol Works, Bristol.   *The most powerful aerospace company in Europe*

Flight March 6th 1969
Ad Ref 41485

216

Interavia March 1969
Ad Ref 82207

The world is about to be halved
in size

Concorde

BRITISH AIRCRAFT CORPORATION | SUD-AVIATION FRANCE
100 PALL MALL LONDON SW1 | 37 BOUL DE MONTMORENCY PARIS 16e

Flight March 13th 1969
Ad Ref 41486

218

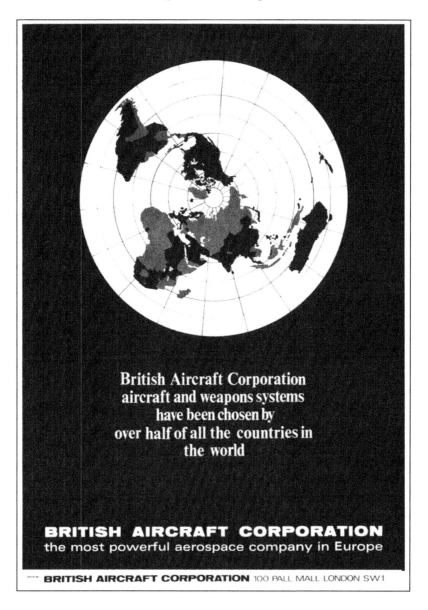

Air Pictorial April 1969
Ad Ref 4879

1968 – First flight of the JAGUAR 01 prototype two-seat trainer on September 8 at Istres.
Prototype 02 built.
The other prototypes, including the tactical single-seater, in an advanced stage of construction.

1969 – Seven prototypes, representing four of the five versions of the JAGUAR, will participate in the accelerated flight test programme.

1970/1971 – The different versions of JAGUAR will complete the flight test programme.

First deliveries of 400 JAGUARS ordered by the French and UK Governments will be made to L'Armée de l'Air and the Royal Air Force.

JAGUAR – The most effective of the advanced super-'sonic tactical support and training aircraft of the 1970s.

S.E.P.E.C.A.T
Société Européenne de Production de l'Avion E.C.A.T.

Breguet Aviation
78-VELIZY-VILLACOUBLAY, FRANCE

British Aircraft Corporation
100 PALL MALL, LONDON, S.W.1.

Interavia April 1969 Ad
Ref 82213

220

Flight April 10th 1969
Ad Ref 41490

221

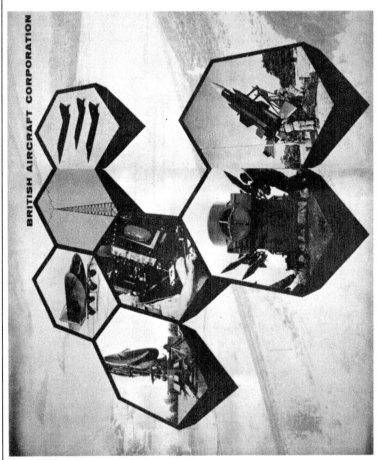

Integrated
Air Defence
Systems

The Guided Weapons Division of British Aircraft Corporation is concerned with so much more than weapons. And so much more than weapon systems. They think systematically certainly but in terms of fully integrated defence systems. The complete package, in fact.

Guided Weapons Division not only supply and install the systems but also offer full back-up services, including personnel training and initial maintenance in the early stages of operation.

BAC Air Defence Systems based on the Rapier and Thunderbird anti-aircraft systems are highly flexible and mobile. They provide both early warning and tactical control for missiles and fighter aircraft.

BAC's full-scale capability was recognised last year when it won from Libya Britain's biggest ever contract for air defence systems.

BRITISH AIRCRAFT CORPORATION

The most powerful aerospace company in Europe

Guided Weapons Division
Stevenage Herts England

Flight April 17th 1969
Ad Ref 41495

BRITISH AIRCRAFT CORPORATION
leaders in European collaboration

Concorde — BAC and Sud-Aviation of France

Jaguar — BAC and Breguet Aviation of France

Intelsat IV — BAC, as the main subcontractor to Hughes Aircraft Corporation of the USA, is working with nine European aerospace firms.

MRCA — BAC and Messerschmitt-Bolkow of Germany, Fiat of Italy, and Fokker of the Netherlands.

BRITISH AIRCRAFT CORPORATION
the most powerful aerospace company in Europe

Flight May 29th 1969
Ad Ref 41484

In 1968 our salesmen travelled 2,500,000 miles overseas...

...and sold £75,700,000 of aerospace products for Britain

1968 was not a flash in the pan – and that is why today over half of all the countries of the world have chosen BAC aircraft or weapon systems. It has taken many years of work and investment to establish for BAC products and after-sales service the level of international reputation and acceptance once enjoyed only by the biggest American manufacturers. Aerospace is probably the most rapidly expanding of all the world markets, and BAC is proud to have created, at the right time, both the products and the environment in which they can be sold.

BRITISH AIRCRAFT CORPORATION
the most powerful aerospace company in Europe

100 PALL MALL LONDON SW1

BAC 300

Air Pictorial August 1969
Ad Ref 4890

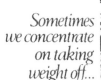

Flight August 14th 1969
Ad Ref 41492

We plan for the safety of just one pair of men...

Seebac spheres made by BAC enlarge the radar echo area of liferafts, small boats etc to guide rescue aircraft

...and for the safety of whole nations

Rapier, BAC's latest anti-aircraft weapon system, will play a vital part in the defence system of Libya as well as that of the British armed forces.

Seebac spheres and Rapier missiles are both products of advanced technology but there any resemblance ends – save that both are made by British Aircraft Corporation. The spheres are compact structures; defence systems – like the one BAC is providing in-Libya – are multi-million pound complexes for which BAC co-ordinates the work of many specialist companies as well as of its own factories. Contrasts like this typify the great span of activity which is one of BAC's strengths. Its products range from specialised plastics to missile systems; from subsonic and supersonic airliners to space satellites; and from high-performance military aircraft to industrial equipment. No other aerospace company in Europe can match the variety of BAC's activities, capabilities, and technical and commercial achievements.

 BRITISH AIRCRAFT CORPORATION
the most powerful aerospace company in Europe
100 PALL MALL LONDON SW1

BAC

Flying Review September 1969
Ad Ref 41494

We provide means
of improving
a telephone call
between neighbours...

Automatic Test Equipment developed
by BAC is being used to test elements
of new automatic telephone exchanges

...and of holding 6,000 simultaneous telephone conversations
between nations half the world apart

BAC and its European associates will build two and make equipment for three of the four Intelsat IV satellites
which will meet increased global communications needs in the 1970s.

These are two ways in which British Aircraft Corporation is making telling contributions to the improvement of national and international communications. Both
provide evidence of the far-reaching influence on world technology of the great
aerospace groups like BAC. BAC's leadership extends across the entire spectrum
of aerospace engineering, from sophisticated equipment and instruments to space
satellites, subsonic and supersonic airliners, advanced missile systems, and high-
performance military aircraft. Over the whole of this broad sweep of activity, BAC
has achieved technical and commercial success beyond the capabilities of any
other European aerospace company.

BRITISH AIRCRAFT CORPORATION
the most powerful aerospace company in Europe

100 PALL MALL LONDON SW1

BAC 306

Flight September 11th 1969
Ad Ref 41493

In 1968/69
our salesmen
have travelled
over 5,000,000 miles
overseas...

...and sold £253,400,000 of aerospace products for Britain

1968/69 was not a flash in the pan — and that is why today over half of all the
countries of the world have chosen BAC aircraft or weapon systems. It has taken
many years of work and investment to establish for BAC products and after-sales
service the level of international reputation and acceptance once enjoyed only by
the biggest American manufacturers. Aerospace is probably the most rapidly expanding of all the world markets, and BAC is proud to have created, at the right
time, both the products and the environment in which they can be sold.

 BRITISH AIRCRAFT CORPORATION
the most powerful aerospace company in Europe
100 PALL MALL LONDON SW1

BAC 300 A

Flight October 23rd 1969
Ad Ref 41489

Sometimes our achievement is the maintenance of a gap of one-millionth of an inch...

...sometimes the halving of the distances of the world

In British Aircraft Corporation, a talent for microscopic perfection of detail is combined with the broad sweep of thinking which advances the state of world technology. It is this depth of ability and resource which has brought BAC technical and commercial success across the whole range of aerospace activity. This extends from supersonic and subsonic airliners to intricate instruments and from high-performance military aircraft to advanced missile systems and space satellites. Alone among Europe's aerospace companies, BAC is accepted beyond Europe's frontiers as one of the decisive influences on the patterns of development and the pace of progress.

BRITISH AIRCRAFT CORPORATION
the most powerful aerospace company in Europe
100 PALL MALL LONDON SW1

Flying Review November 1969
Ad Ref 41491

229

British Aviation Industry Advertisements

Some of our products are designed for one flight in a lifetime...

Over 200 Skylark rockets have been successfully launched to probe the earth's atmosphere up to heights of 190 miles

...others to take off and land somewhere in the world every minute of the day and night

BAC One-Eleven jet airliners are in service with over 30 operators throughout the world

Skylark and BAC One-Eleven are part of British Aircraft Corporation's product range, which extends from space satellites to precision instruments, from subsonic and supersonic airliners to advanced military aircraft and missile systems. The two projects have one quality in common: success. Skylark is one of the most successful of all space probes. The One-Eleven is the only European jet airliner to have penetrated American-dominated markets, including the USA itself, in depth. Products like these have made BAC Europe's most experienced space engineering company, with a major share in such projects as the 11-nation Intelsat IV programme, and the world's most widely experienced manufacturers of turbine-powered airliners, with an unrivalled 10,500,000 hours of flight experience.

 BRITISH AIRCRAFT CORPORATION
the most powerful aerospace company in Europe
100 PALL MALL LONDON SW1

BAC 304

Flight November 6th 1969
Ad Ref 41487

230

For Europe's biggest aircraft programme
Europe's biggest aerospace combine

In Panavia, the immense resources of technology, skill and experience of **Messerschmitt-Bolkow-Blohm, Fiat and British Aircraft Corporation** have been brought together to design, develop and produce for Europe an outstanding multi-role combat aircraft
Panavia has been chosen by the governments of Germany, Italy and Great Britain to provide the spearhead of their new Air Power
This great programme will add immeasurably to the defensive, industrial and technological strength of Europe

PANAVIA AIRCRAFT GMBH. MÜNCHEN, ARABELLA STRASSE 16-22, GERMANY

The sure way to safeguard the future of Europe

Flight November 13th 1969
Ad Ref 41590

231

You could take this picture any day at almost any of the airports of more than fifty countries. It's a BAC One-Eleven landing after a scheduled service or a holiday flight, or a charter operation, or an international business journey. It could have come from only 100 miles away—or from 1,600 miles. Inside could be up to 109 passengers or just a handful of top company men in an airborne executive suite. Whatever its mission, this BAC One-Eleven is backed by four years of successful airline service and by an active development programme run by the world's most experienced team in the short-haul business.

The Rolls-Royce engined jetliners of the One-Eleven family meet the sternest requirements in the toughest field of all civil aircraft engineering. They do it with a profitability, economy and reliability which have been proven under almost any conditions you care to name.

BAC ONE-ELEVEN

BRITISH AIRCRAFT CORPORATION
the most powerful aerospace company in Europe

100 PALL MALL LONDON SW1

Flight November 20th 1969
Ad Ref 41488

Flight December 11th 1969
Ad Ref 41591

Flight March 12th 1970
Ad Ref 40539

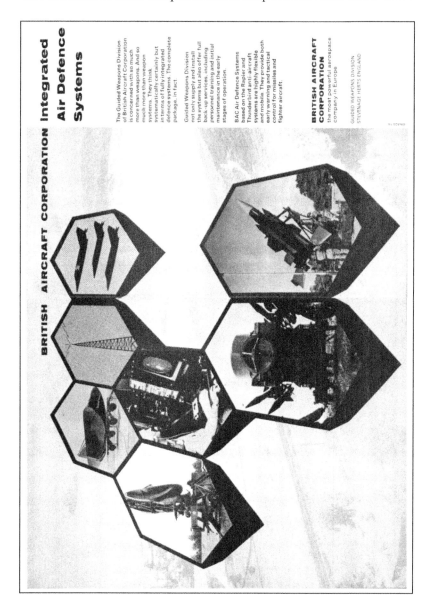

Flight March 12th 1970
Ad Ref 40547

We provide means
of improving
a telephone call
between neighbours...

Automatic Test Equipment developed
by BAC is being used to test elements
of new automatic telephone exchanges

...and of holding 6,000 simultaneous telephone conversations
between nations half the world apart

BAC and its European associates will build two and make equipment for three of the four Intelsat IV satellites
which will meet increased global communications needs in the 1970s.

These are two ways in which British Aircraft Corporation is making telling contributions to the improvement of national and international communications. Both
provide evidence of the far-reaching influence on world technology of the great
aerospace groups like BAC. BAC's leadership extends across the entire spectrum
of aerospace engineering, from sophisticated equipment and instruments to space
satellites, subsonic and supersonic airliners, advanced missile systems, and high-
performance military aircraft. Over the whole of this broad sweep of activity, BAC
has achieved technical and commercial success beyond the capabilities of any
other European aerospace company.

BRITISH AIRCRAFT CORPORATION
the most powerful aerospace company in Europe
100 PALL MALL LONDON SW1

BAC 306

Flight March 12th 1970
Ad Ref 40548

236

better than predicted
for achieved flight speeds – Concorde has already flown for sustained periods at speeds above Mach 1.5, compared with the speed of Mach 1.3 earlier programmed for this phase of testing.

better than predicted
in supersonic flight exploration – so satisfactory has aircraft handling been that it has been possible to extend investigation of the supersonic and transonic flight envelope beyond the limits initially foreseen.

better than predicted
in aircraft serviceability – in 12 months since first flight, more than 100 flights totalling over 200 hours and including some 30 hours' supersonic flying have been completed by two aircraft, all but 24 of the flights being by prototype 001.

better than predicted
in engine performance – the Rolls-Royce/SNECMA Olympus turbojets have far exceeded performance predictions, although the definitive engines have not yet been fitted and only fixed-geometry air intakes have been used.

better than predicted
in flight test progress – not only has the supersonic and transonic flight envelope been explored in greater depth than initially programmed, but pilots of four major airlines have been able to make their first evaluation of Concorde.

Concorde

AEROSPATIALE (SNIAS) FRANCE & BRITISH AIRCRAFT CORPORATION

better than predicted

Flight March 26th 1970
Ad Ref 40541

237

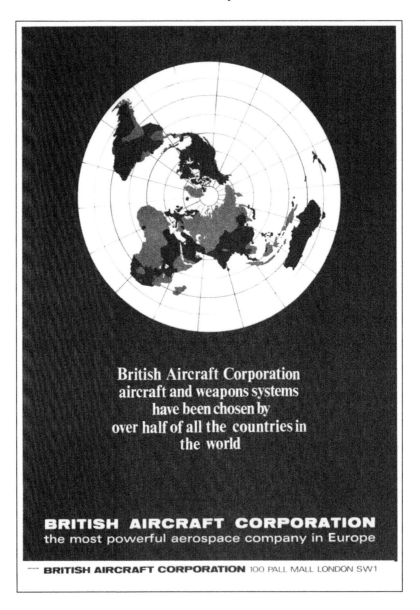

Air Pictorial April 1969
Ad Ref 4879

The sure way...
is by united effort

The demands of Europe's biggest and most advanced aircraft programme have called into being Europe's biggest aerospace combine. The Panavia multi-role combat aircraft is backed by the immense resources and skills of the **British Aircraft Corporation, Messerschmitt-Bolkow-Blohm and Fiat**. Not only will this ensure that the Air Defence Forces of Great Britain, Germany and Italy will be spearheaded by the finest equipment yet devised : it will add overwhelmingly to the defensive, industrial and technological strength of Europe.

PANAVIA AIRCRAFT GMBH, MÜNCHEN, ARABELLA STRASSE 16-22, GERMANY

The sure way to safeguard the future of Europe

Flight April 2nd 1970
Ad Ref 40612

239

British Aviation Industry Advertisements

Supersonic Jaguar

By a considerable margin, the most modern and cost effective warplane in production today

- Two hundred ordered for Great Britain, two hundred for France
- Weapon load of 4,500 kg, plus good radius of action
- High-accuracy, self-contained, unjammable navigation/attack system
- Excellent short-field performance for tactical operations
- Specific design for high-speed, low-altitude tactical operations
- Twin-engined safety
- Ease of maintenance plus low running costs
- Docile handling qualities and low approach speed make Jaguar especially suitable for militia pilots
- Single-seat and two-seat configurations developed

Designed and built by

S.E.P.E.C.A.T. BRITISH AIRCRAFT CORPORATION and BREGUET AVIATION

Flying Review May 1970
Ad Ref 40544

240

Flight May 28th 1970
Ad Ref 40542

Some of our
aircraft are built
to meet one
specialised need...

The BAC 221 was built for research into slender
delta wingforms and has provided valuable data
for the Concorde

...most to meet worldwide requirements

Designed and built jointly by BAC and Breguet Aviation of France, Jaguar will meet world needs for a supersonic trainer and close-support aircraft in the 1970s

The BAC 221 was a one-off experimental aircraft built for a highly specialised
purpose. Jaguar, however, is designed for a worldwide market throughout the
1970s, and already five versions are being built to initial British and French orders
for 400 aircraft. Meeting such extremes of requirement is part of the fabric of
British Aircraft Corporation's working life. Unremitting research underlies all its
activities, from high-performance military aircraft to supersonic and subsonic
airliners; from advanced missile systems and space satellites to precision instruments. But the end-purpose is always commercial as well as technical success.
Alone among European aerospace companies, BAC has achieved that commercial
success on the scale needed to win a place among the handful of international
companies shaping the future of aerospace development.

 BRITISH AIRCRAFT CORPORATION
the most powerful aerospace company in Europe

100 PALL MALL LONDON SW1

BAC 303

Flight June 4th 1970
Ad Ref 40543

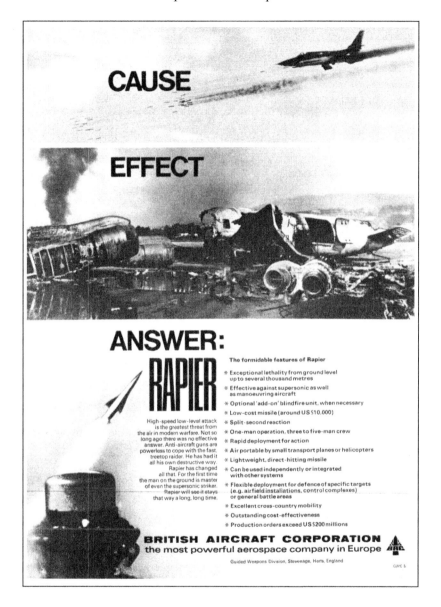

Flight June 4th 1970
Ad Ref 40545

*Sometimes our achievement
is the maintenance
of a gap of
one micron...*

In miniature high-precision gyros produced by BAC, separations between faces are often as little as one micron.

...sometimes the halving of the distances of the world

Concorde, designed and built by BAC and AEROSPATIALE (SNIAS) France, will bring New York within 3½ hours of London, Tokyo within 8½ hours of Los Angeles

In British Aircraft Corporation, a talent for microscopic perfection of detail is combined with the broad sweep of thinking which advances the state of world technology. It is this depth of ability and resource which has brought BAC technical and commercial success across the whole range of aerospace activity. This extends from supersonic and subsonic airliners to intricate instruments and from high-performance military aircraft to advanced missile systems and space satellites. Alone among Europe's aerospace companies, BAC is accepted beyond Europe's frontiers as one of the decisive influences on the patterns of development and the pace of progress.

 BRITISH AIRCRAFT CORPORATION
the most powerful aerospace company in Europe

100 PALL MALL LONDON SW1

BAC 301A

Flight June 18th 1970
Ad Ref 40540

NATO prizes the Lightning over all other fighters

British Aircraft Corporation congratulates No. 5 Squadron of the Royal Air Force Strike Command, flying Lightning interceptors, on winning the 1970 Huddleston Trophy – NATO's award to its top fighter squadron.

Each year, NATO fighter squadrons and their associated ground control stations compete in realistic tests designed to prove each air defence sector's efficiency. Over a period of two months in 1970, Lightnings,

Mirages, F-104s and F-102s flown by pilots of eight Allied nations completed more than 200 sorties under representative operational conditions – by day and by night, in good weather and bad, at subsonic and supersonic speeds.

And No. 5 Squadron, with its Lightnings, outflew all the other contestants in this international test of air defence efficiency and fighter performance which faithfully simulates the realities of actual combat.

LIGHTNING

designed and built by

BRITISH AIRCRAFT CORPORATION
the most powerful aerospace company in Europe

Flight July 16th 1970
Ad Ref 40538

245

We plan
for the safety
of just one
pair of men...

Seebac spheres made by BAC enlarge the radar echo area of liferafts, small boats etc to guide rescue aircraft

...and for the safety of whole nations

Rapier BAC's latest anti-aircraft weapon system, revolutionises the concept of battlefield defence and is now in production for the British armed forces

Seebac spheres and Rapier missiles are both products of advanced technology but there any resemblance ends – save that both are made by British Aircraft Corporation. The spheres are compact structures; defence systems are multi-million pound complexes for which BAC co-ordinates the work of many specialist companies as well as of its own factories. Contrasts like this typify the great span of activity which is one of BAC's strengths. Its products range from specialised plastics to missile systems; from subsonic and supersonic airliners to space satellites; and from high-performance military aircraft to industrial equipment. No other aerospace company in Europe can match the variety of BAC's activities, capabilities, and technical and commercial achievements.

 BRITISH AIRCRAFT CORPORATION
the most powerful aerospace company in Europe

100 PALL MALL LONDON SW1

BAC 30

Flying Review September 1970
Ad Ref 40546

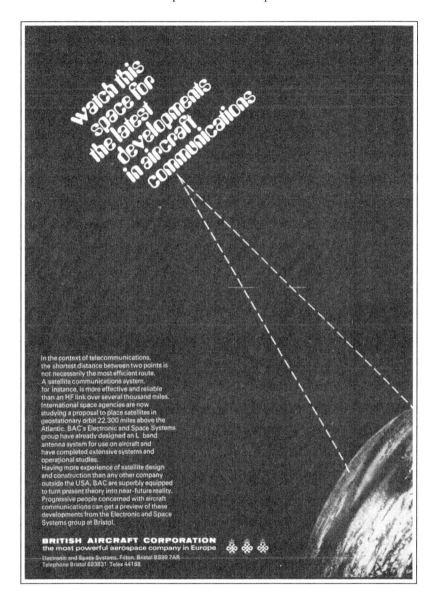

Flight September 17th 1970
Ad Ref 56709

Flight September 17th 1970
Ad Ref 56710

Is this jet approaching Cowra or Chicago?

At either airport – up-country in Australia, or in the 'Windy City' on the shores of Lake Michigan – the 74/89-seat BAC One-Eleven 475 will be completely at home.

The One-Eleven 475 is a jet which can bring to country-town citizens all over the world the same big-jet standards and amenities which the big cities have long enjoyed.

The One-Eleven 475 will operate at full load from runways as short as 4,000 ft, even those with unsealed surfaces or poor load-bearing characteristics. It is profitable for a series of hops as short as 100 miles, or for smooth, 550 mph sectors up to 1,500 miles.

A brand-new jet – but backed by a depth of experience no competitor can rival. It is derived directly from the latest One-Eleven 500 which it can partner in the airline inventory of the '70s to make jet service really universal.

The BAC One-Eleven 475 features improved aerodynamics, increased Rolls-Royce power, advanced landing gear design. It is in production and on programme for airline service next year.

BAC One-Eleven 475 – the jet to keep profits constant through all the variations of traffic flow and airport standards.

COWRA, New South Wales, Australia: population; 7,082; airport, 5,300 ft., sealed surface strip.
CHICAGO, Illinois, U.S.A.: population, 3,550,404; airport, O'Hare, 11,600 ft. runway.

BRITISH AIRCRAFT CORPORATION
the most powerful aerospace company in Europe
100 PALL MALL LONDON SW1

Flight October 22nd 1970
Ad Ref 56711

249

Interavia November 1970
Ad Ref 77025

what

means ...

PANAVIA *means the three-nation company which is building Europe's next-generation multi-role combat aircraft.*

PANAVIA *means a multi-project alliance between three of Europe's largest and most experienced aerospace companies.*

PANAVIA *means fulfilling European military requirements from within European resources.*

PANAVIA *means three countries sharing research and development costs and increasing production runs to achieve maximum cost-effectiveness.*

PANAVIA *means harnessing the skills and experience of the aerospace leaders of three European nations.*

PANAVIA *means the combined resources of* **Messerschmitt-Bölkow-Blohm, Fiat** *and* **British Aircraft Corporation.**

PANAVIA builds MRCA
Europe's solution to Europe's defence

PANAVIA AIRCRAFT GMBH, München, Arabellastrasse 16-22, Germany   PVABA

Air Pictorial December 1970
Ad Ref 4766

251

Flight December 10th 1970
Ad Ref 56733

We plan
for the safety
of just one
pair of men...

Seebac spheres made by BAC enlarge the radar
echo area of liferafts, small boats etc to guide rescue
aircraft

...and for the safety of whole nations

Rapier BAC's latest anti-aircraft weapon system revolutionises the concept of battlefield defence and is now in production for the British armed forces

Seebac spheres and Rapier missiles are both products of advanced technology but there any resemblance ends – save that both are made by British Aircraft Corporation. The spheres are compact structures; defence systems are multi-million pound complexes for which BAC co-ordinates the work of many specialist companies as well as of its own factories. Contrasts like this typify the great span of activity which is one of BAC's strengths. Its products range from specialised plastics to missile systems; from subsonic and supersonic airliners to space satellites; and from high-performance military aircraft to industrial equipment. No other aerospace company in Europe can match the variety of BAC's activities, capabilities, and technical and commercial achievements.

 BRITISH AIRCRAFT CORPORATION
the most powerful aerospace company in Europe
100 PALL MALL LONDON SW1

BAC 305 A

Flight January 21st 1971
Ad Ref 56808

Air Pictorial February 1971
Ad Ref 4950

We provide means
of improving
a telephone call
between neighbours...

Automatic Test Equipment developed by
BAC is being used to test elements of new
automatic telephone exchanges

...and of holding 6,000 simultaneous telephone conversations
between nations half the world apart

BAC principal contractor to Hughes Aircraft Company and its European associates
will build two and make equipment for three of the four Intelsat IV satellites which will meet increased global communications needs in the 1970s

Intelsat IV satellites are being built by BAC, as principal overseas contractors to Hughes Aircraft Company,
for the International Telecommunications Satellite
Consortium. The programme is directed by the
Communications Satellite Corporation, acting as
manager for the Consortium, comprising 68 member
nations.

These are two ways in which British Aircraft Corporation is making telling contributions to the improvement of national and international communications. Both
provide evidence of the far-reaching influence on world technology of the great
aerospace groups like BAC. BAC's leadership extends across the entire spectrum
of aerospace engineering, from sophisticated equipment and instruments to space
satellites, subsonic and supersonic airliners, advanced missile systems, and high-
performance military aircraft. Over the whole of this broad sweep of activity, BAC
has achieved technical and commercial success beyond the capabilities of any
other European aerospace company.

BRITISH AIRCRAFT CORPORATION
the most powerful aerospace company in Europe
100 PALL MALL LONDON SW1

Flight February 18th 1971
Ad Ref 56809

255

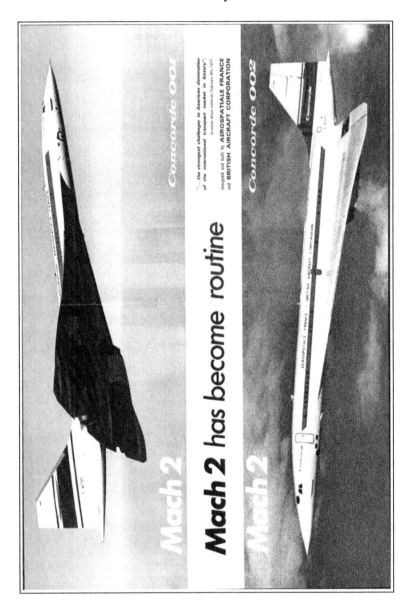

Flight April 15th 1971
Ad Ref 56810

Flight April 29th 1971
Ad Ref 56812

257

Flight May 20th 1971
Ad Ref 56813

Flight June 10th 1971
Ad Ref 56814

The right place for ALL instruction is in the cockpit

The right place for pre-flight instruction is the cockpit of the trainer itself, where instructor and pupil can see and handle the same instruments and controls. Side-by-side seating in the BAC 167 Strikemaster and Jet Provost Mk 5 makes that possible. Both instructor and pupil have the unrestricted forward view – not to be had with existing tandem-seat aircraft in this category – that is essential for ground attack and weapons training, reconnaissance etc. It is one of the design features – confirmed by over 1m hours' flying experience – which make these the most practical and cost-effective jet trainers in production. The Royal Air Force and eight overseas air forces – in New Zealand, Africa, the Middle East and Far East – are already basing pilot-training for the 1970s on the Jet Provost Mk 5 and Strikemaster. Communication between instructor and pupil is direct and unambiguous. And the advantages carry right through to operational use of the Strikemaster in the ground attack role.

BRITISH AIRCRAFT CORPORATION
the most powerful aerospace company in Europe
100 PALL MALL LONDON SW1

Flight June 24th 1971
Ad Ref 56815

260

Today

BAC One-Eleven, Lightning, BAC 167 Strikemaster and Thunderbird are among the aircraft and missile systems which have made BAC a world force in aerospace

the value of BAC products
in worldwide service is $3,500,000,000

Tomorrow

The BAC/Breguet Jaguar, the Panavia MRCA, the Rapier missile system, and space programmes such as Intelsat IV provide a broad and international base for BAC's drive for larger world markets

The Concorde supersonic airliner, designed and built by BAC in collaboration with Aérospatiale of France, will revolutionise the world's long distance air travel

we will double it.

BRITISH AIRCRAFT CORPORATION
the most powerful aerospace company in Europe
100 PALL MALL LONDON SW1

Air Pictorial July 1971
Ad Ref 4956

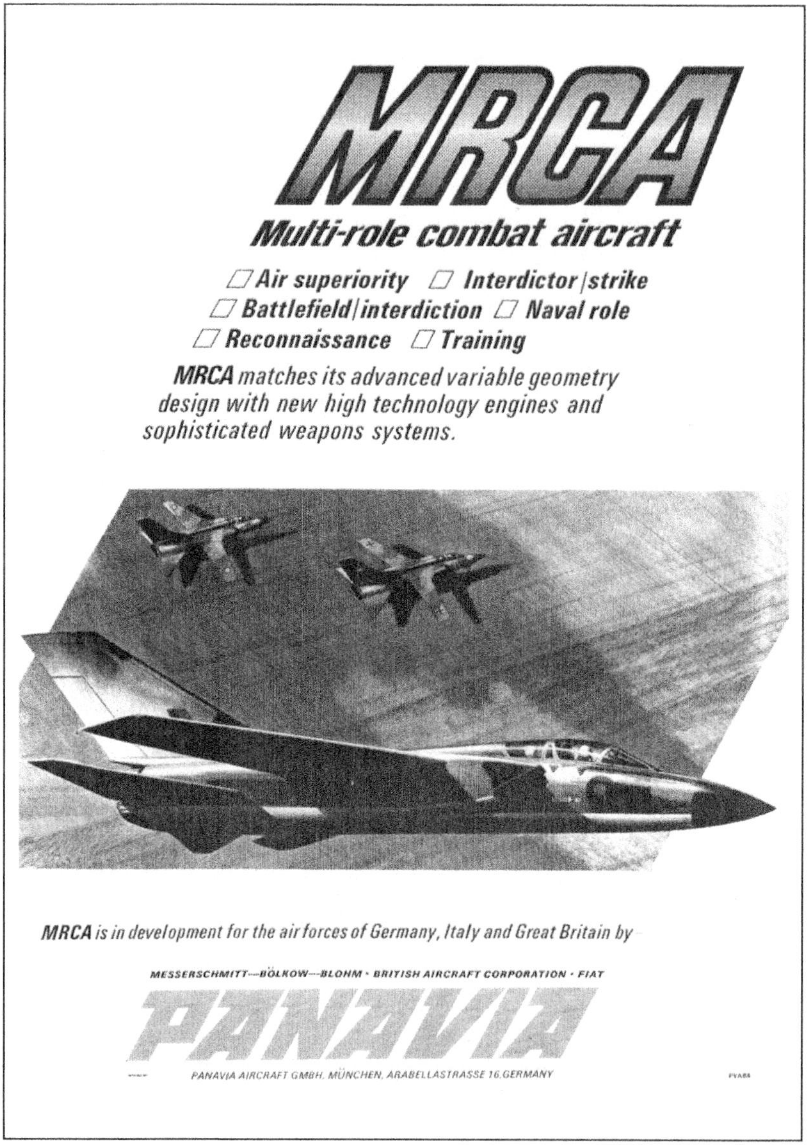

Air Pictorial September 1971
Ad Ref 4982

NATO's top interceptor

for the third year running

Royal Air Force pilots of No 5 Squadron, flying Lightnings built by British Aircraft Corporation, have again proved themselves NATO's top interceptors by winning the annual fighter unit competition in which RAF squadrons compete for the Huddleston Trophy against Allied units flying combat aircraft such as the US Phantom.

BRITISH AIRCRAFT CORPORATION
the most powerful aerospace company in Europe
100 PALL MALL LONDON SW1

Flight September 2nd 1971
Ad Ref 56816

Flight September 30th 1971
Ad Ref 56817

Flight November 18th 1971
Ad Ref 56818

265

British Aviation Industry Advertisements

Flight November 25th 1971
Ad Ref 56896

Air Pictorial December 1971
Ad Ref 4945

Nine air forces have found one cost-effective solution to their requirements... the versatile, adaptable BAC 167 Strikemaster

Proven performance, linked with high survival capability in service with nine air forces, is resulting in re-orders of the BAC 167 Strikemaster aircraft. Its versatility has led to its adoption for duties ranging from basic pilot training, through operational conversion and weapons training, to tactical strike. With instructor and pupil side by side in a pressurised cockpit, the Strikemaster is the proven, safe, robust and efficient answer to modern air force needs. Dual optical gunsights and ability to carry a variety of weapon loads make it the ideal trainer in which to learn both to fly and to fight.

As a tactical strike aircraft, the Strikemaster operates with a full weapon and fuel load from hot and high airfields and grass or laterite-surfaced strips. In active service, it has repeatedly proved its ability to survive retaliatory ground fire. Eight carrying points ensure flexibility of choice in weapon and fuel loads, and guns installed in the fuselage are carried on all missions.

With its low purchase price and low operating and maintenance costs, the BAC 167 Strikemaster is a cost-effective addition to both training and fighting strength.

BRITISH AIRCRAFT CORPORATION
the most powerful aerospace company in Europe
100 PALL MALL LONDON SW1

BHP 3

Interavia January 1972
Ad Ref 77165

Air Pictorial April 1972
Ad Ref 5050

270

Flight April 27th 1972
Ad Ref 57046

Air Pictorial June 1972
Ad Ref 5085

272

Air Pictorial July 1972
Ad Ref 5081

The most cost-effective military aircraft in production today

■ Four hundred ordered for Great Britain and France ■ Weapon load of 4,500 kg, plus good radius of action ■ High-accuracy, self-contained, un-jammable navigation/attack system ■ Excellent short-field performance for tactical operations ■ Specific design for high-speed low-altitude tactical operations ■ Twin-engined safety ■ Ease of maintenance combined with low running costs Single-seat strike and two-seat operational trainer versions.

Designed and built by
S.E.P.E.C.A.T.
BRITISH AIRCRAFT CORPORATION and AVIONS MARCEL DASSAULT/BREGUET AVIATION
100 PALL MALL, LONDON, S.W.1.   B.P. 32 92 VAUCRESSON FRANCE
JAG 24

Flight August 3rd 1972
Ad Ref 57092

Flight August 17th 1972
Ad Ref 57047

Flight August 31st 1972
Ad Ref 57048

Air Pictorial September 1972
Ad Ref 5066

Air Pictorial November 1972
Ad Ref 5089

Air Pictorial December 1972
Ad Ref 5040

Air Pictorial January 1973
Ad Ref 5153

A Skylark rocket being launched from the BAC/RAE transportable launcher to be used in an Earth Resources survey programme in Argentina.

BAC success in Space

BAC shared in the design, assembly and testing of all four Intelsat IV communications satellites which today link the world's main population centres.

Intelsat IV and Skylark have demonstrated the breadth of capability which has won British Aircraft Corporation clear leadership in European space technology. In the 11-nation Intelsat IV programme directed by the Communications Satellite Corporation, BAC was main overseas contractor to the Hughes Aircraft Company and was responsible for the first commercial satellite ever assembled outside the USA. Skylark, with a background of 300 successful launchings, has now been developed into an Earth Resources research instrument of world importance.

BAC now has over a decade of space satellite experience, starting with equipment built for the early Anglo-US spacecraft. It built the first all-British satellite, Ariel III, and its successor, Ariel IV, and played a leading role on ESRO's HEOS satellites and Britain's first technology satellite, PROSPERO. Current programmes include the 9-nation STAR Consortium's GEOS satellite, programmed for launch in 1976, and the technical study, with Hughes, of still larger communications satellites.

BRITISH AIRCRAFT CORPORATION

BAC 332

100 PALL MALL LONDON SW1

Flight February 8th 1973
Ad Ref 57199

Air Pictorial March 1973
Ad Ref 5170

The British Aircraft Corporation Aerospace Adverts 1960-1977

British Aircraft Corporation designs and builds leaders in Defence and every field of Aerospace. **Rapier** has revolutionised missile defence against treetop aircraft attacks. **Swingfire** has changed the balance of power in defence against armoured attacks. The new surface-to-air **Seawolf** and air-to-surface **CL834** helicopter-borne system continue this leadership in missile engineering. **Jaguar** with Dassault/Breguet is the most cost-effective tactical support aircraft in production today. **MRCA** with MBB of Germany and Aeritalia is Europe's most important military aircraft. **Strikemaster** has been chosen by nine nations for ground attack and training. **Concorde** with Aérospatiale France will halve the world in size. **One-Eleven 475** brings mainline jet services to the small fields. **Europlane** with Saab-Scania of Sweden, CASA of Spain and MBB will bring the boon of quiet take-off and landing to the world's airports. And in **Space,** too. BAC has established the same position of leadership as in every other field of Aerospace.

BRITISH AIRCRAFT CORPORATION
100 PALL MALL LONDON SW1

Flight April 12th 1973
Ad Ref 57200

283

British Aviation Industry Advertisements

British Aircraft Corporation designs and builds leaders in every field of Aerospace. **Concorde** with Aerospatiale France will halve the world in size with supersonic services; **One-Eleven 475** brings mainline jet services to the small fields. **Europlane** with Saab-Scania of Sweden, MBB of Germany and CASA of Spain will bring the boon of Quiet Take-Off and Landing to the world's airports. **Jaguar** with Dassault/Breguet is the most cost-effective tactical support aircraft in production today; **MRCA** with MBB and Aeritalia is Europe's most important military aircraft, while **Strikemaster** has already been chosen by nine nations for ground attack and training. **Rapier** has revolutionised the concept of missile defence against tree-top aircraft attacks, just as **Swingfire** has changed the balance of power in the ground fight against tanks. We can say little of the surface-to-air **Seawolf** and helicopter-borne air-to-surface **CL834** weapon systems, save that each is a world leader in its class. BAC's **Space** programmes are, beyond challenge, the most successful in Europe and include BAC teamwork on **Intelsat IV** with Hughes Aircraft and on the **Space Shuttle** with North American Rockwell.

BRITISH AIRCRAFT CORPORATION
100 PALL MALL LONDON SW1

Air Pictorial May 1973
Ad Ref 5173

284

The British Aircraft Corporation Aerospace Adverts 1960-1977

Flight June 14th 1973
Ad Ref 57201

285

Where you can take a DC3,

you can take a **BAC One-Eleven 475**

Taking jet travel to routes hitherto restricted to propeller-driven aircraft was the task for which the BAC One-Eleven was specifically developed. On scheduled airline services in South America, the Pacific and Africa, the One-Eleven 475 has conclusively demonstrated that jet speed and jet comfort are no longer contingent upon costly capital investment in airport facilities. Operating from unsurfaced runways – such as that at Ayacucho, Peru, shown in the photograph above – the One-Eleven 475 is consistently profitable over journeys as short as 100 miles or as long as 1,500 miles. And it operates from these "country" airfields without sacrifice or the quality and amenity of comfort which make it equally at home on the most competitive international routes and with the most experienced and sophisticated travellers.

Leadership with the BAC One-Eleven 475

▲ **BRITISH AIRCRAFT CORPORATION**
100 PALL MALL LONDON SW1

BAB-421

Flight June 28th 1973
Ad Ref 57202

286

Air Pictorial July 1973
Ad Ref 5157

MRCA
is bringing together the strength of three European nations

MRCA PRODUCT OF EUROPE

MRCA is on programme in the factories of Great Britain, Germany and Italy.

Production of some 800 aircraft is already planned.

MRCA will equip the British, German and Italian air forces and the German Navy.

It will fill six vital front-line roles.

MRCA is the first European programme directed by a specially appointed tri-lateral NATO organisation, NAMMO.

It is being carried out by a tri-national industrial consortium, Panavia.

MRCA mobilises the experience and resources of Europe's leading equipment and systems specialists.

Britain, Germany and Italy are all contributing to research, design, development, production and flight testing.

MRCA meets the defence needs of the late 1970's and beyond.

MRCA will have its first flight early in 1974.

◁ Main Airframe Contractors
◁ Airframe & Equipment Sub-Contractors
▭ Main Engine Contractors
▭ Engine Sub-Contractors

AERITALIA
BRITISH AIRCRAFT CORPORATION
MESSERSCHMITT-BÖLKOW-BLOHM

Panavia Aircraft GmbH, München, Arabellastrasse 16, Germany

PVA12

Air Pictorial July 1973
Ad Ref 5159

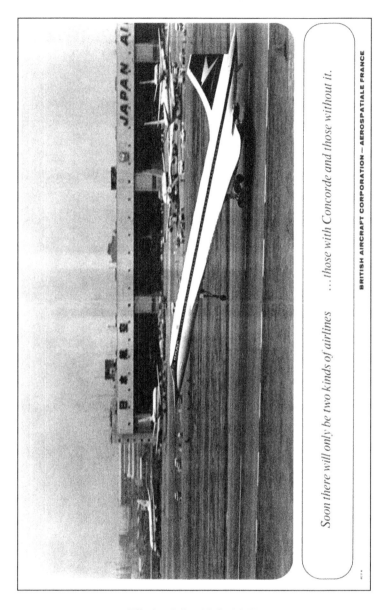

Flight July 12th 1973
Ad Ref 57203

289

Impression of the Europlane QTOL Airliner.

British Aircraft Corporation has won leadership in every field of Aerospace, both civil and military. **Europlane QTOL** – with MBB of Germany, Saab-Scania of Sweden and CASA of Spain – will bring the boon of quiet take-off and landing to the world's airports. **One-Eleven 475** brings mainline jet service to the small fields. **Concorde** – with Aerospatiale France – will halve the world in size. **Jaguar** – with Dassault/Breguet – is the most cost-effective tactical support aircraft in service or production today. **MRCA** – with MBB and Aeritalia – is Europe's most important military aircraft. **Strikemaster** has been chosen by nine nations for ground attack and training. **Rapier** has revolutionised missile defence against treetop aircraft attacks. **Swingfire** has changed the balance of power in defence against armoured attacks. The new surface-to-air **Seawolf** and air-to-surface helicopter-borne **Skua** systems continue this leadership in missile engineering. And BAC has leadership, too, in many **Space** projects.

BRITISH AIRCRAFT CORPORATION
100 PALL MALL LONDON SW1

BAC 139

Flight August 16th 1973
Ad Ref 57204

The British Aircraft Corporation Aerospace Adverts 1960-1977

Air Pictorial September 1973
Ad Ref 5180

291

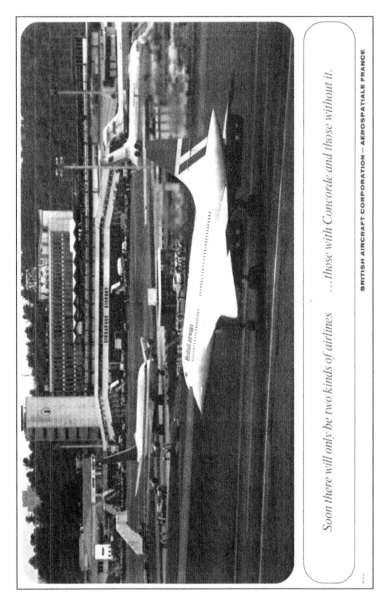

Flight September 27th 1973
Ad Ref 57205

The World's most
cost effective
warplane is now
in service ...

---jaguar

A7

SEPECAT
JAGUAR

Designed and built by S.E.P.E.C.A.T. | BRITISH AIRCRAFT CORPORATION 100 Pall Mall, London, S.W.1.
AVIONS MARCEL DASSAULT/BREGUET AVIATION B.P. 32 92 Vaucresson, France.

Flight September 27th 1973
Ad Ref 57329

No matter how you look at the world, over half of all the countries have chosen aircraft and weapons designed and built by **BRITISH AIRCRAFT CORPORATION** 100 PALL MALL LONDON SW1

Flight October 4th 1973
Ad Ref 57206

294

The British Aircraft Corporation Aerospace Adverts 1960-1977

Flight December 13th 1973
Ad Ref 57207

British Aviation Industry Advertisements

Leadership is our heritage

1 GUNBUS   5 S6B   9 SPITFIRE   13 CANBERRA   17 VC10   20 JAGUAR
2 F28 FIGHTER   6 WELLESLEY   10 BEAUFIGHTER   14 VISCOUNT   18 LIGHTNING   21 ONE-ELEVEN
3 VIMY   7 WALRUS   11 VIKING   15 VANGUARD   19 JET PROVOST   22 CONCORDE
4 BULLDOG   8 WELLINGTON   12 VALIANT   16 BRITANNIA   & STRIKEMASTER   23 MRCA

BRITISH AIRCRAFT CORPORATION
100 PALL MALL LONDON SW1

Flight December 13th 1973
Ad Ref 57208

296

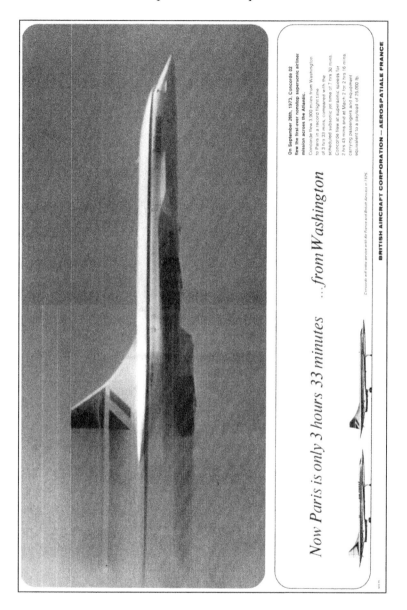

Flight December 13th 1973
Ad Ref 57209

British Aviation Industry Advertisements

Air Pictorial January 1974
Ad Ref 1581

The British Aircraft Corporation Aerospace Adverts 1960-1977

The choice of 9 air forces — and three of them have re-ordered

Nine air forces in South America, Africa, Asia, Australasia and the Middle East have to date ordered BAC Strikemaster aircraft – and three have placed repeat orders, making a total of 120 Strikemasters so far purchased by overseas nations.

Development of the Strikemaster was funded entirely by British Aircraft Corporation. This rugged and versatile aircraft meets, at low cost, today's need for genuine multi-role capability, combining pilot and weapons training with operational strike and reconnaissance.

Carrying weapon loads of up to 3,000 lb (1,360 kg), in addition to integral armament of two machine guns, Strikemasters have proved their efficiency and reliability in operation in the heat, sand and dust of desert and mountain terrains, as well as in more temperate environments.

Outstanding operational characteristics ensure a continuing demand for the Strikemaster, and a continuing production programme ensures early availability of aircraft to meet future new export orders.

Leadership with the **BAC STRIKEMASTER**

BRITISH AIRCRAFT CORPORATION
Military Aircraft Division, Warton Aerodrome, Preston, Lancs.

Flight January 24th 1974
Ad Ref 57468

299

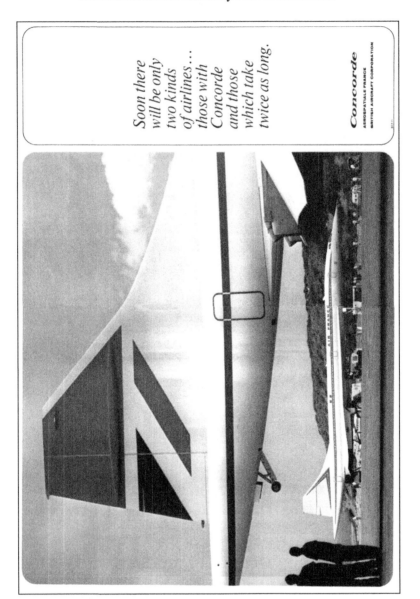

Soon there
will be only
two kinds
of airlines...
those with
Concorde
and those
which take
twice as long.

Concorde
AEROSPATIALE FRANCE
BRITISH AIRCRAFT CORPORATION

Flight March 21st 1974
Ad Ref 57469

The British Aircraft Corporation Aerospace Adverts 1960-1977

British Aircraft Corporation is in the very vanguard of progress in civil and military aviation, guided weapons and in Europe's key Space projects. **Jaguar** – with Dassault/Breguet – is the most cost effective tactical support aircraft in service or production today. **MRCA** – with MBB of Germany and Aeritalia – is Europe's most important military aircraft. **Strikemaster** has been chosen by nine nations for ground attack and training. **Rapier** has revolutionised missile defence against treetop aircraft attacks. **Swingfire** has changed the balance of power in defence against armoured attacks. The new surface-to-air **Seawolf** and air-to-surface **Sea Skua** helicopter-borne system continue this leadership in missile engineering. **Concorde** – with Aerospatiale France – will halve the world in size. **One-Eleven 475** brings mainline jet services to the small fields. And in many **Space** and satellite projects, too, BAC has Leadership.

BRITISH AIRCRAFT CORPORATION
100 PALL MALL LONDON SW1

Air Pictorial April 1974
Ad Ref 1580

301

British Aviation Industry Advertisements

Flight April 25th 1974
Ad Ref 57470

Air Pictorial May 1974
Ad Ref 1569

No1

... for Europe's defence

The first of some 800 MRCA aircraft scheduled to be
built for the British, German and Italian defence forces.

... for cost-effectiveness

MRCA is, by a large margin, cheaper to buy and to
operate than any other projected aircraft in its field.

PANAVIA

Panavia Aircraft GmbH, München, Arabellastrasse 16, Germany

AERITALIA
BRITISH AIRCRAFT CORPORATION
MESSERSCHMITT-BÖLKOW-BLOHM

Air Pictorial June 1974
Ad Ref 1606

304

Air Pictorial August 1974
Ad Ref 1579

British Aviation Industry Advertisements

The choice of
9 air forces —
confirmed by
6 re-orders

Nine air forces in South America, Africa, Asia, Australasia and the Middle East now operate BAC Strikemaster aircraft – and, in 1974 alone, three have re-ordered, bringing the number of repeat orders to six and the total of aircraft ordered by overseas operators to 134.

Development of the Strikemaster was funded entirely by British Aircraft Corporation. This rugged and versatile aircraft meets, at low cost, today's need for genuine multi-role capability, combining pilot and weapons training with operational strike and reconnaissance.

Carrying weapon loads of up to 3,000 lb (1,360 kg), in addition to integral armament of two machine guns, Strikemasters have proved their efficiency and reliability in operation in the heat, sand and dust of desert and mountain terrains, as well as in more temperate environments.

Outstanding operational characteristics ensure a continuing demand for the Strikemaster, and a continuing production programme ensures early availability of aircraft to meet future new export orders.

Leadership with the BAC STRIKEMASTER

BRITISH AIRCRAFT CORPORATION
Military Aircraft Division, Warton Aerodrome, Preston, Lancs.

BKP34

Flight August 15th 1974
Ad Ref 57471

Air Pictorial November 1974
Ad Ref 1567

The world's most cost-effective warplane is in service with two air forces and on order for two more...

... *Jaguar*

Designed and built by **S.E.P.E.C.A.T.**

BRITISH AIRCRAFT CORPORATION
100 PALL MALL, LONDON, S.W.1.
AVIONS MARCEL BREGUET / DASSAULT AVIATION
B.P. 32 92 VAUCRESSON FRANCE

Air Pictorial December 1974
Ad Ref 1568

Flight December 5th 1974
Ad Ref 57472

Flight March 13th 1975
Ad Ref 57789

Flight March 20th 1975
Ad Ref 57790

Jaguar – now in service with two air forces – has
set new standards of accuracy in low-level attack

worldbeaters

BAC 364 / 2 / 75

JAGUAR –low-level tactical strike and reconnaissance aircraft
built by BAC and Dassault/Breguet

CONCORDE –supersonic intercontinental airliner
built by BAC and Aérospatiale

MRCA –multi-role combat aircraft
built by BAC, Messerschmitt-Bölkow-Blohm and Aeritalia

RAPIER –ultra-low-level missile air defence system
built by British Aircraft Corporation

...each at the top of its class

BRITISH AIRCRAFT CORPORATION
the spearhead of technological achievement
100 PALL MALL LONDON SW1

Air Pictorial May 1975
Ad Ref 1633

312

Supremacy From the tree tops
to the stratosphere...
for defence
or interdiction...
for complete
performance in all
weathers at the
lowest cost...
the MRCA is
the outstanding
aircraft of
this decade.

Panavia Aircraft GmbH, München, Arabellastrasse 16, Germany
AERITALIA
BRITISH AIRCRAFT CORPORATION
MESSERSCHMITT-BÖLKOW-BLOHM

Flight May 29th 1975
Ad Ref 57918

313

British Aviation Industry Advertisements

Flight May 29th 1975
Ad Ref 57954

314

Flight June 5th 1975
Ad Ref 57791

Flight June 12th 1975
Ad Ref 57792

Supremacy From the tree tops
to the stratosphere...
for defence
or interdiction...
for complete
performance in all
weathers at the
lowest cost...
the MRCA is
the outstanding
aircraft of
this decade.

PANAVIA MRCA

Panavia Aircraft GmbH, München, Arabellastrasse 16, Germany

AERITALIA
BRITISH AIRCRAFT CORPORATION
MESSERSCHMITT-BÖLKOW-BLOHM

Flight August 28th 1975
Ad Ref 57919

317

Flight October 2nd 1975
Ad Ref 57794

319

Flight October 23rd 1975
Ad Ref 57795

Flight November 6th 1975
Ad Ref 57796

Flight November 20th 1975
Ad Ref 57797

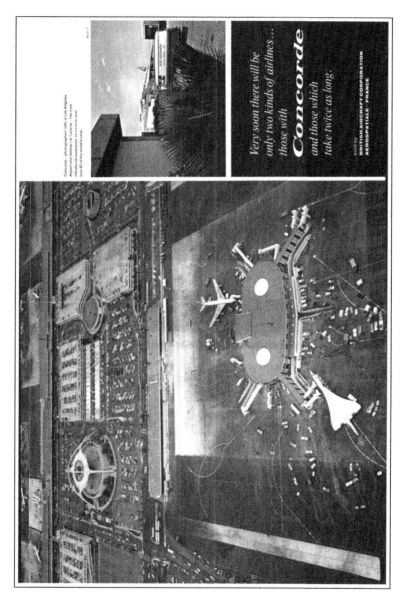

Flight December 4th 1975
Ad Ref 57798

We build more than just products

We build leadership. We are one of the handful of international aerospace companies whose work shapes technological progress.

We build confidence. Our products, chosen by over half of all the countries in the world, are backed by after-sales services second to none.

We build international partnerships. We have greater experience than any other company in the world of collaboration with other nations on high-technology programmes.

We build technological capability. We are constantly probing the frontier of knowledge on programmes which cover the whole span of aerospace technology.

We build experience. For more than 60 years we have been continuously involved in the design, development, production and world-wide marketing of military and civil aircraft and, more recently, missiles, space satellites, and associated equipment and systems.

We build Concorde *(with Aerospatiale of France)*
MRCA *(with MBB of Germany and Aeritalia of Italy)*
Jaguar *(with Dassault/Breguet of France)*
BAC One-Eleven
Strikemaster
Rapier
Swingfire
Seawolf
Intelsat IV and IVA satellites and sub-systems *(with Hughes Aircraft Company of USA)*
GEOS *(as leader of the 14-company STAR consortium)* and a constantly developing range of high-technology products for use in the air, on land, at sea, and in space.

BRITISH AIRCRAFT CORPORATION
100 PALL MALL LONDON SW1

Air Pictorial January 1976
Ad Ref 5193

Air Pictorial January 1976
Ad Ref 5194

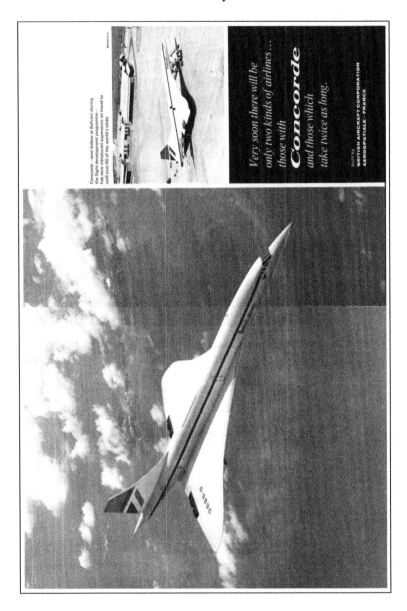

Concorde – seen below at Bahrain during the flight development programme – has now introduced supersonic air travel to well over 60 of the world's cities.

Very soon there will be only two kinds of airlines ... those with **Concorde** and those which take twice as long.

built by
BRITISH AIRCRAFT CORPORATION
AEROSPATIALE – FRANCE

Flight January 17th 1976
Ad Ref 58250

326

Flight February 14th 1976
Ad Ref 58184

Flight May 1st 1976
Ad Ref 58251

Even airstrips like this can now be jet cargo airports with the...

new convertible BAC One-Eleven 475

The BAC One-Eleven 475 has proved that it combines reliability and exceptional fuel efficiency with the ability to operate from 4,000ft low-strength runways and unsealed and gravel strips. Now it is available as a quickly convertible passenger/cargo aircraft with a hydraulically powered freight door measuring 3.05m x 1.83m and capable of accepting international-sized pallets. The operator simply removes as many seats as necessary to obtain the desired cargo volume and puts in a freight-floor overlay, complete with longitudinal roller sections and ball mats. This new facility, which also extends the domain of the One-Eleven into military transportation, can be fitted retrospectively to any of the 220 and more BAC One-Elevens today in service with over 60 operators worldwide.

BRITISH AIRCRAFT CORPORATION
100 PALL MALL LONDON SW1

Flight May 8th 1976
Ad Ref 58252

329

Air Pictorial June 1976
Ad Ref 5200

Nine air forces in the Middle East, Africa, Asia, Australasia and South America now operate BAC Strikemaster aircraft – and five of those air forces have given the best possible proof of their satisfaction by placing, between them, a total of 10 re-orders, bringing the total overseas orders to 145 aircraft.

Development of the Strikemaster was funded entirely by British Aircraft Corporation. This rugged and versatile aircraft meets, at low cost, today's need for genuine multi-role capability, combining pilot and weapons training with operational strike and reconnaissance.

Carrying weapon loads of up to 3,000 lb (1,360 kg), in addition to integral armament of two machine guns, Strikemasters have proved their efficiency and reliability in operation in the heat, sand and dust of desert and mountain terrains, as well as in more temperate environments.

Outstanding operational characteristics ensure a continuing demand, for the Strikemaster, and a continuing production programme ensures early availability of aircraft to meet future export orders.

BAC STRIKEMASTER

BRITISH AIRCRAFT CORPORATION
Military Aircraft Division, Warton Aerodrome, Preston, Lancs.

Flight June 26th 1976
Ad Ref 58253

Flight June 26th 1976
Ad Ref 58315

In "appalling" weather...

A Jaguar of No 14 Squadron of the Royal Air Force which put up the best individual performance in the Salmond Trophy navigation and bombing competition arrived dead overhead of target, dead on time, and scored a direct hit. The weather was officially described as "appalling".

Jaguar – the best tactical strike aircraft in existence.

jaguar Designed and built by **S.E.P.E.C.A.T.**

BRITISH AIRCRAFT CORPORATION
100 PALL MALL, LONDON, S.W.1
AVIONS MARCEL DASSAULT/BREGUET AVIATION
B.P. 32 92 VAUCRESSON FRANCE

Flight September 4th 1976
Ad Ref 58186

333

Air Pictorial October 1976
Ad Ref 5215

334

Air Pictorial November 1976
Ad Ref 5212

335

Air Pictorial January 1977
Ad Ref 5234

The British Aircraft Corporation Aerospace Adverts 1960-1977

Flight January 1st 1977
Ad Ref 58634

337

The more expensive fuel becomes...

the more you gain with the **BAC One-Eleven**

The BAC One-Eleven is one of the world's most fuel-efficient airliners. It is certificated for automatic landing and, although proven in over 10 years of worldwide operation, still represents the most advanced standards of structural design. More than 200 One-Elevens are today making over 7,000 flights each week to destinations in more than 60 countries and maintaining a record of reliability unlikely to be bettered by any jetliner in its class.

BAC One-Eleven today's best value in its class

BRITISH AIRCRAFT CORPORATION

100 PALL MALL LONDON SW1

Flight April 9th 1977
Ad Ref 58522

338

The British Aircraft Corporation Aerospace Adverts 1960-1977

The BAC One-Eleven has proved itself one of the world's most consistently profitable and reliable airliners. The One-Eleven 500 is the most fuel-efficient jetliner in the 100-seater category. It is certificated for automatic landing, and the latest production version has "hush kits" which satisfy ICAO annex 16 noise regulations. Although proven in over 10 years of worldwide operation, the One-Eleven still represents the most advanced standards of structural design, with a structure which can be cleared through to 60,000 flights without major re-work. More than 200 One-Elevens are today making over 7,000 flights each week to destinations in 63 countries throughout the world, maintaining an average dispatch reliability of 98-99 per cent – a fine record for any short/medium-haul jet airliner.

BAC One-Eleven 500
today's best value in its class
BRITISH AIRCRAFT CORPORATION
Weybridge Surrey England

British Aircraft Corporation, a ***BRITISH AEROSPACE*** *company*

Flight May 28th 1977
Ad Ref 58523

339

Air Pictorial June 1977
Ad Ref 5240

Air Pictorial June 1977
Ad Ref 5241

Some air forces will have
an unfair advantage ...

The advantage of the West's first truly multi-role, multi-mission, Mach 2+ weapons system.

The advantage of air-to-air self-defence capability and advanced defensive electronic aids, plus short-field performance permitting operation from small, dispersed airfields.

The advantage of all-weather, night-and-day, long-range, high-speed, high-precision, automatic terrain-following strike and reconnaissance capability.

PVA 28 B

PANAVIA

Panavia Aircraft GmbH, München, Arabellastrasse 16, Germany

AERITALIA
*BRITISH AIRCRAFT CORPORATION
MESSERSCHMITT-BÖLKOW-BLOHM
*British Aircraft Corporation is a British Aerospace company

TORNADO

Air Pictorial December 1977
Ad Ref 5229

342

Some air forces will have an unfair advantage ...

The advantage of the West's first truly multi-role, multi-mission, Mach 2 + weapons system.

The advantage of all-weather, night-and-day, long-range, high-speed, high-precision, automatic terrain-following strike and reconnaissance capability.

The advantage of air-to-air self-defence capability and advanced defensive electronic aids, plus short-field performance permitting operation from small, dispersed airfields.

TORNADO

PANAVIA
Panavia Aircraft GmbH, München, Arabellastrasse 16, Germany

AERITALIA
'BRITISH AIRCRAFT CORPORATION
MESSERSCHMITT-BÖLKOW-BLOHM
'British Aircraft Corporation is a British Aerospace Company

Flight December 3rd 1977
Ad Ref 58635

343

British Aviation Industry Advertisements

For latest compilations please visit
www.aviationancestry.co.uk

Printed in Great Britain
by Amazon